The Firing Line

Liz Newton was born in Australia, has three adult children and currently lives in Sydney with her husband and dog.

Extensive travelling – including road trips across continents, sailing adventures and family holidays – has provided inspiration for creative writing and photography.

Liz has worked in health services and, in particular, mental health, including drug and alcohol, in a variety of roles, as well as teaching and tutoring at universities and involvement in health research and ethics.

Her academic background is in Anthropology and Comparative Sociology. Research has included exploring issues of indigenous suicide, vocational training opportunities for people with mental health issues, and a PhD doctoral thesis on the ethnography of deinstitutionalisation for people with mental illness, resulting in many peer reviewed publications.

More recently, Liz has enjoyed the freedom and creativity of fiction writing, and has published two novels, *Faraway on an Island* and *Jagged Edge of Joy*, as well as *Meandering*, a selection of short stories some of which have won awards in competitions. This is her first memoir.

Fiction by Liz Newton
Faraway on an Island
Meandering: Collected Stories
Jagged Edge of Joy

Liz Newton

The Firing Line

A memoir of a family ablaze

For my mother, brother, sister and father (deceased)

Disclaimer

This memoir reflects the author's memory and recollection of events, which is supported by research and perusal of medical records. Names of some family members have been changed to protect their privacy.

The Firing Line: A memoir of a family ablaze
ISBN 978 1 76041 749 9
Copyright © text Liz Newton 2019
Cover photo: Skully MBa

First published 2019 by
GINNINDERRA PRESS
PO Box 3461 Port Adelaide 5015
www.ginninderrapress.com.au

Contents

1	A Strange Place	7
2	Early days of illness	15
3	A Memorable New Year's Eve	25
4	Life without a window	30
5	Sea Glass	39
6	Magical days	44
7	In the firing line	48
8	My birthday wish	53
9	Peaks and troughs	60
10	Fires	65
11	'The times they are a-changin' (Dylan 1964)	69
12	Teenage runaways	73
13	'School's out for summer' (Alice Cooper, 1972)	79
14	Moving on	84
15	The Ha Ha wall	92
16	Chimera	97
17	Dad's death	102
18	Looking back	107
19	Bittersweet	110
	References and Notes	115
	Acknowledgements	117

1

A strange place

Mine is a story often told – the yearning for something better, the longing to leave the past behind. Yet history of course, never escapes you. It may lie dormant and may not bother you, except for tiny twinges from a skewered heart, but eventually it meets you again. On an ordinary day decades later in 2016, I felt my past acutely. It resurfaced in a place I had long forgotten.

The weeping willow trees still lined the damp creek banks in the psychiatric hospital's spacious grounds. I could see, though, that they had thinned out over the last fifty years since my childhood. Recalling how I swung from the branches all those years ago sent a tingle of exhilaration through my veins.

Usually I walked back to work from the local shops at lunchtime via the footpath rather than cross-country. Drawn to linger, today a slight chill hung in the air, a remnant from winter just passed. My senses were tantalised with the smell of freshly mown grass and new buds as spring bloomed. Sun rays peeked through the clouds as I walked through the hospital grounds.

Detouring toward the willows, I strolled under the canopy, an umbrella of dangling wisps. Childhood days resonated as I imagined swinging with my brother Johnno and sister Jane from the long thin branches. We had spun and jumped to see who could go the furthest and highest. I fleetingly felt the same childhood temptation although, now much older, thought better of it. Commonsense told me not to try it – the branches probably wouldn't take my adult weight. Instead, I sat for a while. Alone. There were some good days, I recalled, even in that weird place. We'd swing from the willows before stripping the branches to create whips, pretending to be cowboys and play rodeo games, which filled many hours.

Wistful, I closed my eyes, surprised at how easily thoughts of past times emerged. Thud. A vague memory of being barred from playing in the willows filtered back. We were made aware of the tragedy in the willow trees. In my mind, an image emerged of a shape obscured through the dappled light above, which led to the grass where one white sandal lay. Higher up, the other sandal was secured to a woman's foot. A drooping head, a face draped by lanky blonde hair, feet about a foot or so off the ground. A gentle breeze swayed a limp body from a twine rope.

When no longer allowed in the willow tree area, along with my brother and sister we looked for tadpoles and frogs in the creek before heading back to Fraser House. This was the therapeutic community ward where our father had been admitted, along with our mum, who also stayed overnight as part of the treatment program to help Dad.

At the time of the woman's death, staff hurried to the wooded grove. An ambulance had been called and two men whisked her away as discreetly as possible before other patients of the hospital noticed while out walking, or those ward-bound glared through the windows. News travelled fast between the wards.

Fraser House was unusually subdued in the evening, I recalled. 'Thank God it's quiet,' I said out loud, before quickly looking around to make sure no one heard me. Hoping for a reprieve from the Big Group therapy session was what pleased me most – maybe we could go home early with Nanna, who was minding us in our home. Perhaps she'd turn on the telly and let us watch our favourite shows before bed. We might even catch the end of *The Flintstones*.

In hushed tones, others heard of the woman's tragedy. She had lived a couple of streets away from our home and coincidentally had also been a patient in the same hospital as our father. The woman's son, a snowy haired boy, found it hard to get on with the other boys at school. He was about twelve and teased because his accent was difficult to understand. I recalled how awful it was for him at the time. No one knew the details of his mother's recent death. Warned not to mention it to the other schoolkids, even though I was busting to tell, I somehow knew it was one of those things best kept quiet.

Lunchtime is over. Time to return to my office.

I looked up at the hill nearby, a verdant contour of mown grass leading up a gentle slope to higher ground. There stood the remains of the now abandoned building, a labyrinth of pastel-coloured corridors and closed doors. Fraser House. What a crazy place that was!

Later, swivelling on my desk chair, I found it difficult to concentrate on work. I was edgy and wondered whether my memories of the ward were real or imagined. Distracted while attempting to rewrite a report, which was due, ideas skittered through my head. Shutting down the computer early, I fabricated a convincing excuse to enable me to escape the office confines. I headed to the library, planning to look into the archives and history of Fraser House.

After obtaining a heap of photocopied information, I tramped through the grass to the willows and settled myself with a highlighter pen ready to examine the wad of articles. After two hours, my mind was in overdrive. I'd uncovered much more than expected. My own memories of over five decades ago were not only confirmed but also magnified.

At that point in time, I was heading for retirement after spending over forty years working in the health field, mainly in mental health and drug and alcohol areas, as both a clinician and manager, and later as an ethnographic researcher for my doctoral thesis.

From a professional position, I tried to make sense of what I was reading in relation to my experiences as a child and the many years our family was affected by the omnipresence of Dad's illness. All of this was overlaid by my years of research and inquiry into various aspects of the system and its many changes throughout history, and recent years researching deinstitutilisation in both Australia and overseas. None of my years working in health services stifled my uneasiness felt from childhood.

The reports I waded through concerning Fraser House reinforced my recollections of the ward. Anger surged from deep within and jolted me. I'd been around long enough to understand why change was necessary and welcomed by many to improve the mental health systems and treatment modalities of bygone years.

I inhaled deeply. *I know now it wasn't like that everywhere…*

Other therapeutic communities of the time, in the late 1960s and early 70s, didn't operate like Fraser House. It was different. I'd read about examples nationally and a couple from the UK and USA, and I could now understand how Fraser House had aspects they didn't.

Experimental somehow? I dared to think

I read further some short passages of an evaluation report written in the mid-1960s of a system, which had operated for the previous five years. I thought it was just the way it was then, the way they did things.

Along with my colleagues, we had all learnt about the history of mental illness and practices of psychiatry over past centuries. It was part of most mental health and psychiatry curricula, and we were glad some things had changed for the better from the old days of institutions.

Therapeutic communities were seen as a way forward to give people and families responsibility and independence. It also reflected the liberal times and legislation changes such as the NSW Mental Health Act of 1958, which replaced the Lunacy Act. (There have been many other changes and amendments to the Act over ensuing years.)

However, Fraser House was more radical than others. While the therapies, groups and milieu may have suited some staff, and worked for some patients, I now detected that whenever there is sweeping change there exists the possibility of collateral damage along the way.

I noted a section from a 1965 paper, which pointed out differences regarding Fraser House following mental health reform, from 1959 onwards. It read,

These developments reflect a worldwide movement towards a more liberal approach to the treatment of mental illness in the post-war period. The changes in State Administration (NSW) allowed the development of Fraser House to be more experimental than originally intended. (Clark, A.W., and N. Yeomans 1965)

This particular therapeutic community operated under some salient points of departure from others cited in my readings. The use of slogans such as 'Relatives and friends cause mental illness', 'No one is sick all through' and the one used most of all, 'Bring it up in the group', still rang in my ears from my childhood.

Those bloody big groups, I sighed and remembered the slogans. Mum and Dad even repeated them, sometimes laughing about the upheaval when they arrived home. It wasn't funny at the time, though. Mum said it was a bit like theatre for the gathered audience watching and interjecting when they felt like it. During those groups I sensed that Mum felt uncomfortable. She later told me that sometimes she was reluctant to go because she didn't want to be verbally attacked by the crowd of patients and staff. She even mentioned it again the other day and she's over ninety now. Her once flame of red curls has now dimmed to a salt and pepper grey, yet her green-amber eyes sparkled up as she spoke.

I now wondered why she attended the groups. It was outrageous to expect people to attend when they felt threatened.

At the time, Mum felt she had to. There was real pressure put upon partners to help the resident/patient get better. Their illness was seen as a social problem and a lot of blame was attributed to the family. Fraser House operated as a place of 'total family therapy', which included my siblings and me, as well as Mum. A sign of the times, I guess.

What I hated most was when the follow-up groups came to our house of an evening after Dad had been discharged. I can still feel those sets of eyes scrutinising my family and me. The strange thing is, when I read about this practice all these years later, it is cited as one way to reduce stigma towards the mentally ill – viewing it as a community problem. In theory it sounds okay, but let me tell you, in those days, Jane, Johnno and I just felt embarrassed. The other kids in our street thought we were weirdoes. They enjoyed watching the comings and goings of a van full of patients and nurses, and the carry-on from our suburban house.

It seemed like the follow-up visits went on forever, though possibly it was just a few years.

I tried to make sense of it and realised sometimes in places such as this particular therapeutic community, often the enthusiasm of the charismatic leader enlists a following and with that comes power. Subsequently a feeling of superiority develops, which manifests into ways and practices sanctioned by some senior staff and the system. Even though they mean well, it can also be damaging for vulnerable people.

Recently I accessed newspaper clippings and articles from the NSW State Library on Fraser House in the 1960s. There are many writings and ideas from the director of the unit at the time. He had encouraged interviews to both health related and mainstream press, to espouse the benefits of this therapeutic community and the suicide-prevention twenty-four-hour phone contact: 'Dial SUI to save your life on WW0285…the staff were very busy talking about "states of woe…"' The article further states, '…the phone number saves 20 depressed lives a week', though I understand this would be difficult to statistically prove (*The Sun*, 11/4/62).

Other articles, however, told a story of different treatment, which would be deemed outrageous by today's standards within a hospital ward for mentally ill patients. For example,

> At a revolutionary new psychoanalysis treatment centre at North Ryde habitual alcoholics and advanced neurotics are handed boxing gloves and told to fight it out…to let off steam…(The Director) also encourages them to criticise one another, and swear at each other, this was in the early days…before female patients were admitted to the ward. (The Sun, 11/4/62)

The Big Group therapy was the treatment I remembered most as a child. Often it was so bizarre I thought I'd imagined it. At the time, while I may not have fully understood group therapy, I was nevertheless left with memories of fear and worry about Mum and Dad. I do recall not wanting to go into the big groups, and sometimes the small family group therapy. I was always on edge waiting for the session to finish.

A magazine article by a journalist who interviewed the director and was subsequently allowed to sit in on a group therapy as an observer, said,

> Group therapy itself is a fairly new thing, almost as remarkable as the sight of patient's children setting off to school through the gates of the hospital.
>
> I saw terrific conflicts of words arise as the group battled its way into sanity. With insight, that would be unbearably cruel in any other place, patients shouted and questioned their way onto each other's minds…and when the group contains people bound to each other by closest blood ties, it is shattering.
>
> Other times children were looked after while married couples were at group – children too small stayed in the sand pit.
>
> … Even some of the psychiatrists who come to see the community, first of its kind in Australia and one of the first in the world, find it 'a hair-raising experience'. The Director's response to that, talks about the social side of medicine. 'It is the turn of psychosocial medicine to cure and prevent illness by treating the loved ones as well as the patient. Medicine must treat all those who carry in their relationships the malignant pattern of life that CAUSES or PERPETUATES illness.' (*Woman's Day*, 1965, from NSW State Library)

Reading some of these articles, where adults and other health professionals also found the system disquieting, revealed that my own feelings as a child were spot-on. They were not imagined, rather an accurate reflection of my experience.

Bamboozled by these thoughts, I decided to put the reports and clippings away for the moment. None of it was covered up, yet I couldn't believe it was lost in such a short period of history…forgotten about. Things moved on pretty fast in those days. By the time I worked in the system in the mid-1970s, it had already changed.

Emotionally drained, I placed a bundle of highlighter-slashed sheets in a folder. Sitting on a park bench I fiddled with the remaining articles. Overhead, currawongs squawked to each other as they protected their nest, which was precariously balanced in a tree branch. A magpie swooped.

A shutter came down. I wasn't sure if I could, or even wanted to, tell my story.

2

Early days of illness

I was very young in the 1950s–1960s when Dad first became ill, and consequently didn't fully grasp what was happening. I could not foresee how things were about to change at home. Before Dad became an inpatient in Fraser House, he had tried for some years to get better with the treatments offered at the time. In the early days, he was given barbiturate-type sedatives and older style antidepressants. Later in the 1950s, pills included Largactil, followed by other psychotropic drugs when they were developed. Although the side effects of these drugs were not pleasant and often debilitating, they were seen as a bit of a miracle in those days, as they enabled some long-term residents to live outside the institutions. Largactil was usually given in shiny white pills. It tinged Dad's tanned skin purplish over many years and caused him to develop a slight tremor. This in turn meant he needed to take other tablets to counteract the side effects.

In an out-of-reach cupboard at home sat a dozen bottles of pills. Dad knew which ones he liked to take and ignored the others. However, when in hospital, it wasn't long before Dad feigned swallowing his medication and hid the tablets in his mouth to dispose of later when no one was watching. The staff of course soon cottoned on to patients who didn't swallow the pills. Hence, Largactil was then given in the form of brownish foul-smelling syrup or an injection. Often Dad's syrup dose seemed to fill half a glass tumbler. Throughout the following years, a kaleidoscope of coloured pills rattled in a little cup given to him three or four times a day.

Dad had been admitted to various psychiatric facilities, some private and some public, which required a lot of Mum's time away from us, visiting him and attending joint meetings with doctors and allied staff. Looking back at Mum's self-sacrifice, I wonder how she kept going. Perhaps because she was always hopeful Dad would improve.

During those years, we spent a lot of time with our father's parents, Nanna and Poppa. Older family and friends knew them as Essie and Eddie. When the household was calm, usually when Dad was in hospital, Eddie and Essie shared snippets of their lives with my brother and sister and me.

Nanna, at age seventeen, had travelled alone and unescorted by boat from London to Australia in 1913. She often voiced her first impression of her new country. 'Well! By the time I had landed here and the liner was securely docked,' Nan recalled, 'I knew that this place could never be anything like the home I'd left.'

Walking down the gangplank into the bustling wharf area of the harbour she recollected how she gasped and felt her heart wrench at the rawness of the town. Sydney was so unlike the London she had left. It lacked a long history, pomp and ceremony, devoid of anything much except for pubs and screeching birds. Nan often had a look of melancholy, and would take a deep breath to smother her feelings. Determined to get on with life she told herself, 'Hard work, that's what I'll do.' Retrieving her luggage from the liner, she looked ahead to set off for the boarding house.

In 1915 she met our once handsome grandfather, who was then a sandy-haired young soldier leading his horse, ready to leave for war on the north African coast.

'What happened then, Nan?' I asked.

'We fell in love and became sweethearts through writing letters for four years of the Great War. I waited and waited, and when Eddie returned, we were married and that was that.' Whenever Nan wanted to close a conversation, she'd say, 'Now, kids, off you go and play – no sitting around indoors while the sun shines.'

Nan remained in Australia until she died in her eighties, and called England home, right up to her death.

Pop's stories were all the more fascinating due to their infrequent telling. As a country boy, he headed to the war recruitment office, along with many other lads who were quick to show off their riding skills with their best-bred horses of the south coast and southern highlands.

Pop returned from the war with all his limbs intact. However, occasionally a vacant look passed his weather-beaten face. At those times, no one could reach him. After nearly four years at the front in north Africa and then at Gallipoli, the proud Light Horseman was no longer the boy who had left Australian shores.

'By the time we had landed over there,' Pop began sweating, 'we were all feeling a bit tense, to say the least. Actually, we were bloody well scared to death.'

My brother Johnno sat fiddling with Pop's unloaded World War I rifle as he polished the bayonet. 'Tell me more, Pop. What happened then?'

Pop swatted a mosquito on his cheek, his mind elsewhere. 'Oh…a bloody nightmare, that's what happened.' He shuddered. 'Maybe it's why they called us Diggers. Because after our landing the few of us left were put to use digging trenches and tunnels – and graves.'

Our grandmother Essie called us from the hinged-open kitchen window. 'Come away, kids, enough badgering, leave your pop alone or his ulcer will be playing up again tonight.' She resumed checking the oven and turning the roast potatoes which were swimming in hot dripping.

Johnno gave her a smile and a wave, and then ignored our grandmother's warning. 'But Pop, what else did you do?'

Pop mused. 'Well, it was like this…me and my mates left home as young lads for the big adventure. Apart from going into the city occasionally, we didn't leave the country rural areas much.'

I joined our older brother, along with Jane, and sat quietly listening to Pop's story.

'I was in the 7th Light Horse Regiment,' Pop continued. 'We loved our horses but as the war went on we felt as sorry for nags as ourselves…all getting skinny and tired. By the time our troop was pulled out of north Africa, we were told to leave them there – the horses would be no use at Gallipoli. No bloody use. Ha! Blaze had been my best mate for years.'

'Did you get to use this gun?' Johnno flicked the sharp metal bayonet in and out of the rifle side.

'You bet I used the gun, and the bayonet – killed anything that threatened my mates or me. In the end, I was left with only one bullet… I'd kept it for my horse.' He choked on his words as tears filled the cracks in his sun-lined face. 'Better than leaving the horses to the bloody Arabs to flog to death.'

I cried when I heard that. 'What did you do then?'

Pop coughed as he cleaned his glasses, suddenly aware that both Jane and I were sniffing and wiping tears from our faces.

'Well, we were pretty hungry, so when I saw a rabbit running by I quickly loaded my gun with two nails I had in my pocket and fired.' Pop grinned. 'The rabbit was pinned to a tree by its ears and we all had a hot supper that night…not as good as your nanna's rabbit pie, though.'

We giggled as Nan called us inside. 'Come now, kids, your dinner's ready.'

Over the years, our grandfather related further fragments of his war stories. These included his days at Anzac Cove in the infantry – without his horse, for which he'd never really had time to grieve – as he left one battle for the next. Others in his brigade also survived Gallipoli, fit enough to leave Turkey for another deployment in the near future.

When Pop finally returned to Australia, he tried to forget it all, eager to get on with his life and leave the war behind. Except I sensed he always found it a struggle. Each year, he braced himself for what he called the 'damned dawn service' and Anzac Day parade, which would again bring it up memories and images of those days.

On the twenty-fifth of April each year, after the dawn service and the big shebang that followed, mateship and two-up games at the pub ensued. The defence forces of the Anzacs gradually morphed into a national legend.

Growing up, we could clearly see that Pop's real scars were those hidden inside him and the other diggers, as they stumbled along George Street with their medals. Bands played and onlookers cheered waving tiny flags. Once he was back home after a few drinks at the pub, and soaking in the afternoon sun, we asked Pop why they made such a fanfare at the Anzac marches.

'I don't know, kids.' Pop grimaced as he twisted his back into a comfortable position. 'It was only a small place, Anzac Cove. Nowhere near as big and beautiful as our beaches. It was deafening when there was gun and cannon fire. Funny thing was, during the rest of the time, it was the quiet and the ordinariness that got to us.'

'How, Pop?'

'Well, the guys we fought against were just boys like us.' He laughed. 'The trenches were so close you could hear the bloody enemy fart on a still night.'

In the early 1950s, Mum and Dad were saving for their own home. Dad was a carpenter by trade and helped with the building, as well working with the NSW Fire Brigade. During some of those years, our family lived with Dad's parents in the Sydney suburb of Artarmon, only a few train stops from the city. Our paternal grandparents owned a modest brick bungalow with a covered-in front veranda for extra indoor space. These homes were typical of the architecture of many post-World War I houses around the area. In later years, factories took over and turned most of the suburb into a light-industrial zone. Before the redevelopment, our maternal grandparents, who we also called Nan and Pop, lived further down the same street and our great-grandmother, who we affectionately called Big Fat Nanna, lived one street to the west – all within walking distance. Hence, Mum and Dad had lived about six houses away from each other as children.

When we weren't travelling by train, our paternal grandparents drove the whole family around in an old Ford Prefect car where each person, except the driver, had a child sitting on their lap. Within the cramped space, I have vague memories of leaning and lurching into each other when the car held on the road around tight corners.

Looking back, I'm sure our entire extended family suffered from a lack of space in the home and the car. The pressure to get out of the grandparents' house and into our own home was perhaps one of the precipitants to episodes of Dad's illness.

When the day finally arrived for us to move, Mum was relieved – though she later recalled, maybe it was not far enough away from her in-laws.

Packed up and ready, we drove to our newly built weatherboard house in North Ryde, an emerging suburb at the time, with a new migrant settlement of mission huts across the road in a vacant paddock. I can't recall exactly how many years we had lived with Nan and Pop, but Mum tells me we moved into our new home when I was about eighteen months old, my sister was a three-week-old newborn and my brother about three and a half.

The location was about twenty minutes away by car and conveniently close for our grandparents to stay overnight and commute between the two houses when their son Rob, our father, was later admitted to various psychiatric hospitals.

We were ensconced in our new home for quite a few years before Dad ended up in Fraser House. All the while, Dad's illness, suicide attempts and unpredictability began to shape our family life. He slowly exhausted the rounds of private psychiatric facilities on the lower north shore of Sydney. Due to his erratic behaviour, which was unable to be contained in the less secure North Shore private hospitals, Dad was transferred to the psychiatric ward of the district general hospital. This was where he spent the last couple of weeks before Christmas in 1961.

On Christmas Eve, Dad had been up most of the night, excited about seeing us open our presents, which would be left under the tree the following morning. He loved to play Santa to Jane, Johnno and me. Dad had been Santa every year since we were born and he was adamant this year was not going to be any different.

From the hospital ward, our father hatched a plan. If only it were morning, he thought, I could see the kids before I'm found and taken back.

We heard Dad's story at daybreak when we woke. The evening before in the hospital, after the nurses had finished their rounds and were busy making a cuppa, Dad seized the opportunity to escape via a locked window he'd jimmied open earlier in the evening. The taxi rank, not far away, luckily had a car waiting. The driver was possibly a bit perplexed at Dad's attire – pyjamas only – but he took the fare anyway. After all, it was Christmas.

Our mum was wary, though not entirely surprised, when she heard the taxi pull up at two a.m. Dad jumped out and banged on the door demanding money for the taxi fare.,

'What's that noise Mummy? Is it morning?' In the darkness I had begun to stir.

'Not yet, darling, shush. Now go back to sleep or Santa won't come.'

As the sun peeped on the horizon, we three children ran to the tinsel-laden tree.

Dad gathered us in his arms. 'Merry Christmas, ho ho ho,' he sang, squeezing us a tad too tightly.

'When did you get home, Daddy?' I asked. 'Mummy said we were going to see you in the hospital later today. I wanted to see the tortoises.'

Emboldened, Dad told his story of the great escape. 'Stone walls do not a prison make nor iron bars a cage,' he repeated ad infinitum. This saying soon became his mantra each time he went AWOL or absconded.

Dad then whispered to us. 'You see, I had to run away to make sure Santa had been. They couldn't keep me away from you lot.'

He tickled and played with us and we giggled and squealed with delight.

'I heard a noise last night, but went back to sleep.' I explained, 'It must have been the reindeers on the roof – see, the carrots are gone.'

Johnno didn't really believe any more, but played along with the fantasy. 'I think Santa's been, because he drank the bottles of beer.' He quickly glanced at our mum, who shrugged, then hung back a little watching the scene unfold, wondering when the fiasco would end.

Very soon after breakfast, the phone rang. Dad overheard Mum's hushed tones as she spoke to the ward nurse.

'Yes, he's here…okay. Just a bit wound up. Can we keep him here until after lunch and I'll bring him back?'

Silence. Dad crossed his fingers, eyes pleading toward Mum.

A discussion took place in the background at the other end of the phone, while Mum was on hold. The staff consulted with the doctor and the decision was reached for Dad to be back soon after lunch or they would send the police – once again he'd been admitted as an involuntary patient under the Mental Health Act.

'Thanks,' Mum replied as her voice quavered, knowing it was now her job to persuade our dad to return – even the staff didn't want hassles on Christmas Day.

I can imagine Mum cajoling our dad, relieved when she finally deposited him after lunch on Christmas day, locked safely behind the ward door. The nurses had told her there was nothing to worry about – he wouldn't be escaping again in a hurry. I knew Mum didn't quite believe them. However, she smiled and nodded when she said goodbye. Dad looked forlorn and lost as he waved. Mum said she felt a slight stab in her heart as she watched the pathetic sight of her once vibrant husband, now back in pyjamas, dragging his feet along the grey-flecked lino floor past the dining room, then round and round the circular courtyard, which held the tortoise pond.

The tortoise pond remained with half a dozen tortoises into the 1980s, after which point it was made into a garden after a patient decided to use a tortoise as a missile to break a window. I remember working there in the 1970s when on a rainy night-duty shift the tortoises would walk across the wet cement courtyard and into the corridor. A very strange trip hazard.

Once outside the building, Mum in her usual stoic way pulled her shoulders back and headed toward the car to get back home. She found us playing happily with our Christmas presents. 'No fighting – thank God,' Mum murmured. 'I can't take much more.'

After Mum had cleaned up the house while Jane and I were in the bath, she brought in the load of washing which she had hung out earlier in the day – great day for drying, sunny with a gentle breeze. It would have been the perfect Christmas Day except for the fracas Dad had created. I suspected Mum was relieved that at least Dad's parents, Eddie and Essie, were away at their holiday cottage up the coast. She later told us she couldn't bear the thought of his mother hounding her about keeping up Dad's medications, while also having to listen to Eddie grumble about his ulcer over every meal.

As kids, we cherished these peaceful periods alone with Mum. Nevertheless, they were not long enough. Mum knew Dad would soon either escape or be well enough to be given 'trial leave' from the ward. When leave was eventually granted, our family was expected to drive two hours north to join our grandparents for a few days holiday at their beach house.

Christmas had been a very long day. Mum was quiet. She'd been reflecting on the day's events since the early hours of the morning. Carrying the laundry basket laden with freshly washed sheets under her arm, she pulled herself up the back steps. 'Time for bed, girls,' she called.

'Why can't we stay up late like Johnno?'

'Because he's older and the man of the house again, now that your father's not here.'

Johnno gave Jane and me a sideways smirk as we slunk off to our bedroom. He liked it when Mum was his only company to watch television later in the evening. It was never a late night, though, as she was always exhausted and had to get up early to repeat the chores all over again.

Our arms were overflowing with Christmas loot when Mum followed us into the bedroom. She picked up on our intention to continue playing with some of our new toys which we'd taken into our beds, so she quickly put the two single-bed bottom sheets on.

'Now lie down, girls, nice and still.'

We giggled. 'We're ready.'

Tired after the day's events, Mum gently laid the top sheets, fresh from the clothesline and still a little warm, followed by pink chenille bedspreads, over each of us. We loved having our beds made while we were in them.

I sniffed hard. 'Mummy, I can still smell the sunshine on the sheets.'

In later years, Mum wondered if it was all worth it as she recalled the early days when she and Dad became engaged. With black hair and grey eyes, he was the most handsome boy in the street – a first grade footy player and the best athlete around, always winning some sort of state or national competition. He was a hard worker and they enjoyed going to dances together with lots of friends. However, those days dwindled fast, as did their friends. Mum often pondered what went wrong over the years to cause Dad's mental illness: why did it happen to him, a man with everything going for him, especially their three little angels tucked up in their beds asleep?

3

A memorable New Year's Eve

Following his Christmas Eve escape, Dad settled down and was granted a few days' 'trial leave' at home before returning as planned, before New Year. Once Dad had returned without incident after this bout of leave, he swallowed his pills without spitting them out and obeyed the ward rules. Hence, he was further given a few hours' leave from the ward to attend a family gathering on New Year's Eve. Most of our socialising since Dad had become unwell centred around relatives. Inevitably, old acquaintances drifted away and neighbours kept a polite distance.

The New Year's Eve celebration was always a fun-filled event when our extended family on Mum's side came together for a party. Lots of friends, music and dancing, and a myriad of cousins, tended to fray Dad's nerves. By late evening, he sat weary in a corner, relieved when Mum said she would take him back to the ward early.

Not long after midnight was celebrated, a well-known incident occurred in the early hours of the morning following New Year's Eve in 1962. Our mother's cousin Marion was later described at the inquest as a 'pretty, weepy girl'. Decades on, when I picture her then, and today, with her once cropped curly brown hair now greyed with age, those words still sum her up.

As the 1950s drew to a close, the early 60s brought the era of sex, drugs and rock and roll. The New Year's Eve party in 1962 was like any other we'd enjoyed in recent years. With a few of my auntie's neighbours, we gathered in the backyard with a selection of vinyl records playing and everyone dancing, between drinking and eating. There were no drugs or sex at our party – that was happening elsewhere.

Ours was a family event, where all the relations gathered, including myself aged eight, my older brother and younger sister, along with our parents and the aunts, uncles and cousins, in a modest brick house at Chatswood. We cousins relished being included in the adult party. Depending on age, ranging from six to eighteen, we gradually succumbed to droopy eyes, and drifted off to sleep in one of the three bedrooms – top and tailing if necessary.

The frivolity and music continued into the night as trays of little green and red coloured pickled onions, cheese and pineapple on toothpicks, and steaming cocktail frankfurts were handed around, along with dips and crinkle-cut chips. Plenty of beer, and alcoholic punch with floating strawberries in a sea of canned fruit salad, washed down the plentiful supper. The kids all knew we were not allowed near the punch – I suspected at the time, though, that my teenage cousins dipped into the glass bowl occasionally.

The night was balmy and stars twinkled under a half-moonlit clear sky. At midnight, the New Year was heralded in when everyone linked arms and sang 'Auld Lang Syne'. We swayed and wished each other happy New Year, as the adults made resolutions, which would be broken within a week. In the early hours of morning, the adults tired. One by one they camped in the backyard, veranda and lounge room, or walked home.

That same night, the youngest cousin of my mother's generation, Marion, who was only twenty-five at the time and unencumbered by children, went further afield with her boyfriend. At a trendier party in Bondi, they danced until three in the morning before heading home by car to Sydney's upper North Shore.

New Year's Day threatened to be a scorcher as the sun rose orange, then blazed yellow in the sky. I woke early with the other young cousins ready for a picnic by the Lane Cove River. We grabbed our cossies and towels and left the rest of the packing and carrying to the adults.

'Let's go to Fairyland,' I shouted. I loved the miniature furniture and tiny toadstools set in the garden of imaginary fairies amongst the riverside bushland. Most of all, the thrill of the flying-fox rope pulley lured me to the Fairyland picnic ground.

'No, let's go to Fuller's Bridge. We can hire canoes and swim there,' Johnno demanded.

The debate between cousins continued until the adults woke. When the house was put back in order and the backyard cleared of bottles and cigarette butts, any leftover food was packed into eskies for the day out. Plenty of beer and ice took up most of the esky space.

Squashed into a few cars, we all headed down Delhi Road, where the decision would be made to go left or right at Fullers Bridge, depending on where the best picnic spot might be. In those days, big family groups met regularly under the shady trees along the Lane Cove River in the parklands. All were decked out with baskets of paraphernalia needed for a full day's fun, including plenty of thick white zinc cream for our noses.

Late morning, as the family neared the bridge with the weir on one side and shady areas on the other, we spotted police cars and reporters with cameras. Many sticky-beaks had begun to gather. The decision to turn toward Fairyland was not possible. Along with other picnickers, we were corralled into the right-hand lane to turn into the park on the weir side of the river.

It wasn't long before everyone learnt about the scandal and deaths following the not-so-sedate swinger's party which had taken place within a short distance of the river the night before.

Around the same time on New Year's Day, we overheard the adults talk about Marion, who'd woken in her parents' house late morning, alerted by a knock on the door. Two policemen explained to her father they needed to speak to his daughter.

We imagined our great-aunt, Marion's mother, fidgeting with her hands and smoothing her apron as our uncle interjected and hurried her into action. 'Don't be a nervous Nelly. Show the policemen to the sitting room while I fetch Marion.'

At that stage, her parents were unaware of the reason for the police visit. However, with an ever present working-class wariness and fear of authority, Marion's father gave his daughter a hasty warning: 'A shut mouth catches no flies, remember that, luv.'

Marion, shy and reserved by nature, found it mortifying answering questions for the police, especially in front of her parents, both of whom always referred to her as a 'good girl'. She was embarrassed to admit she'd only arrived home from the New Year's Eve party as the sunbeams lit the dawn horizon.

She and her boyfriend had detoured on the way home to kiss and canoodle, along with other couples in Lovers Lane near the Lane Cove River. However, as she explained to the police and later at the inquest, it wasn't particularly secluded on the night in question as there were about ten cars with couples. Marion noticed a lone man walking nearby, whom she thought creepy. This sighting along with a single car somewhat away from the others prompted them to go home.

'Never mind, luv.' Her father put his arm around her. 'We know you're a good girl and wouldn't get mixed up with any funny business.'

Later as the police related the news of the event of the previous early hours of the morning to the family, Marion's mother almost collapsed, leaning heavily on her husband for support as she wailed, 'You could have been killed, sweetie. You know how we worry.'

Marion's sojourn at Lovers Lane soon became the most widely publicised secret in the neighbourhood.

The media and the radio quickly picked up on a story which became the front page of the tabloids for weeks. The mystery of the Bogle-Chandler deaths was speculated upon and unravelled. Theories abounded of murder, espionage, swingers' parties, wife-swapping, LSD and other chemical compounds from the scientists of the nearby CSIRO.

In the dark hours of New Year's morning, the tide gurgled out of the silted river as the grey mud bubbled and belched its toxic gas. The naked bodies near the riverbank had been moved a little apart and covered. Later it was discovered that an early walker passing by had shielded the bodies out of modesty. In more recent times, ideas formulated which pointed to pollution and fumes from poisonous gas from the river having drugged the couple into sleep before their death.

Nevertheless, to date, there remains only inconclusive evidence as to the cause of the deaths. Marion was an ordinary girl from the upper North Shore, who was by chance brushed by an extraordinary event. She wished for a simple life in which to marry her sweetheart, but instead found her life exposed and turned upside down. The mystery of the case didn't fade with time. It was in and out of the courts, papers, media and public gaze for years. Our family watched the toll it took on Marion.

It was Geoffrey Chandler (Margaret Chandler's husband), in his book about the Bogle-Chandler case and the inquest, who portrayed Marion as a 'pretty, weepy girl'. There were periods throughout her life when these words fitted aptly as she despaired at having her private life laid bare in the public arena for years after the two deaths on New Year's Eve 1962.

4

Life without a window

In 1963, a week after the New Year's Eve party, our father was once again granted extended leave from the hospital. This time it was to accompany the family on our regular holiday up the coast to the fibro beach house which Dad and Pop had built over the years. Traffic on the winding Pacific Highway north was always congested as cars backed up bumper-to-bumper in the holiday season. For our family, though, the tension of the trip began well before we left our front gate.

'Why can't I sit near one?' I whimpered and settled down to another trip in my life without a window.

'Stop whingeing and be quiet, Liz!' Mum leaned over from her front seat ready to give the next child who moaned a slap on their legs.

Actually, there were lots of windows around the vehicle, but my chance of seeing things was diminished. By craning my neck, and with the right amount of pushing and shoving from the middle of the back seat of the car, I could occasionally get a better view. Whenever I tried, however, there were consequences.

Picture a car with windows – smaller than today's standards – front and back, and two each side to correspond with the four doors of an old car in the 1950s and 60s. A Vauxhall, or Standard Vanguard, or perhaps an FJ Holden. Then picture the typical family of that era. Mum, Dad and three kids – one to replace each parent and one for Australia – to help the nation grow they said. Each had their position. Dad in the driver's seat, Mum in the front, and we kids in the back. My brother Johnno always sat behind Mum, while our sister Jane, daddy's little girl, sat behind our father. I was the middle child, and took the place to match my position in the family – squeezed like a sardine in the centre of the back seat – not willingly, though, and not without a tussle.

When the time to depart for the holiday approached, Mum called. 'Come on, kids, get in the car.'

I raced to secure a window seat. Jane, always a fast runner since she could walk, ran to grab the other rear window seat. I held my ground, pleased that I'd secured one at last, until…

My big brother Johnno inevitably came to my side door and opened it. 'Shove over. Hurry up, Mum's coming.'

'No – I've got the window,' I demanded and held on tight.

When our parents arrived with the final pieces of luggage, water and Mintie lollies for the trip, they voiced their usual warnings: 'Now move over, Liz, and stop being stubborn' followed by 'We're not going until you lot stop fighting – Liz, *please* unlock the door and let Johnno get in.'

Defeated, time after time I did as I was told – in the end, it was the easiest option. If we stopped fighting, we would invariably be given a Mintie, and our contest began to see who could tear the perimeter of the waxy-paper wrapper as thinly as possible, to make the longest unbroken piece. 'I won,' the winner would call, hoping for another lolly soon.

As the car moved off, I sulked while Jane and Johnno sniggered. They each kept quiet in case the car was turned back home and the outing abandoned – which had happened on a number of occasions in the past. Even from a young age I had learnt to be hyper-vigilant in the face of Dad's mood changes – always at the ready to make strategies if plans changed.

The transistor radio crackled once the outskirts of Sydney were reached, signifying the real journey had begun. It started with a game of I spy. This was fun to begin with, though it wore thin after an hour. The game lasted the entire journey as each winner fought to win the chance to nominate the next obscure item to spot. 'I spy with my little eye something beginning with…' In the back middle seat, stuck between my brother and sister, who both hogged the view, I was at a distinct disadvantage playing the game.

'Why can't I swap seats?' I bleated and fidgeted, resulting in being elbowed by each of my siblings to prevent being edged into their window-seat territory.

'Ouch, stop it. Mum, tell them not to push me,' I demanded.

'Shut-up in the back. I can't concentrate,' Dad called.

'Shush, darling, we're nearly there,' our mother placated.

I protested. 'It's not my fault I'm squashed. They won't move over.'

Dad gripped the steering wheel so tight I could see his knuckles whiten. The journey was near its end, and our father by this stage had just about had enough of my griping. Tempers were frayed all round.

As we approached one of the final turn-offs before the holiday shack at Davistown on the Central Coast, Dad swerved suddenly and swore. 'Jesus Christ! I'm not going any further. I need a bloody drink.'

Luckily for me and my siblings, the pub we called into at least had a beer garden. That meant we could sit outside with our parents and have a glass of lemonade, rather than sweltering in the car for hours, which would have been the case if the pub had no outdoor area. Dad sat in the bar sculling more than a few schooners of beer. As the day wore on and sunlight dimmed into dusk, the drinking session hadn't finished. We were restless, so we amused ourselves by jumping from bench to bench, eager to get going. Mum pleaded with Dad to return to the car so we could complete the journey before dark.

Finally, on the road again. 'I spy with my little eye…'

'Stick a sock in it, Liz!'

The remaining few nerve-wracking miles along the windy road was silent. No one dared speak, dreading perhaps that there might be another pub on route to detour into. We arrived at last and stumbled and stretched as we exited the car. Dad's parents greeted us and helped unpack the bags, tools, food and linen. Our grandmother had dinner ready and we children hungrily wolfed down corned beef with white onion sauce, before relishing the shortcrust pastry-topped apple pie with whipped cream – Nan's specialty.

When the household was quiet at last, the ABC radio news over, and soft music playing in the background, Jane, Johnno and I fell into a deep slumber in preparation for the morning of our first day at the beach. Our cossies, towels, buckets and spades were ready at the door for an early exit.

Upon waking at the holiday house at Davistown, a gentle breeze sent a whiff of the sweet smelling jasmine, which covered the entire length of the back fence and dripped tiny flowers onto the grass. Parts of the vine had wilted and gone woody, but mostly it flourished.

During our holidays there, we kids were either in the backyard or being shooed away from the house to play in the park for hours on end. This wasn't because Mum didn't want us around, rather that Dad's nerves were so frazzled it was the only way she could keep the peace at home. What sort of holiday was this!

At the park, we kids would gather jellyfish from amongst the stinky seaweed washed up with the tide. Their slimy translucent forms were slippery to grab hold of. When fully laden, we took our buckets to the merry-go-round and hung the jellyfish on the iron spokes. It was a bit like roulette as we backed our rung, hoping to have the last jellyfish hanging on while my brother swung hard and fast, and round and round. Jellyfish flew everywhere until the last one left stretched and hanging was pronounced the winner. This filled in a bit of time.

Then it was off to the wharf with sunburnt skin scratchy with sand, our bait, hooks and lines ready, and noses sticky with white zinc. The crunch of dried fish gut under out feet on the wooden wharf told us the fish must have been biting. We threw bits of gut into the air for the squawking seagulls to squabble over. We also fished for toads, which were ceremoniously left to blow up in the sun before we stabbed them with the fish knife.

Patches of fish scales glinted in the sunlight like diamonds, and the water lapped gently around the struts of the wharf. We could tell from the flow on the channel marker a little further into the bay whether the tide was running in or out. Fish were always more plentiful on the run in, yet that was often a few hours away. Once we'd exhausted our bait fishing, and catching nothing but toads, we grabbed handfuls of green weed to catch blackfish later when out in the rowboat. Hungry and bored, we headed home.

Raised voices and banging from our veranda could be heard from a couple of houses away. The front door was closed so we ventured around the back to the rear door.

Mum heard us coming and quickly met us before we entered. She gave my brother a shilling coin. 'Now skedaddle. Your dad's not well. Buy a lolly each and don't come back until it's dark.'

In those days, we spent many hours without any adult supervision, and we needed to stick together. Off we went again after rinsing our buckets with the tap from the outdoor corrugated-iron tank. We meandered to the park via the dusty lane where the lone grocery shop operated. The money bought us a Choo-choo bar each and some rainbow balls. The Choo-choo bars blackened our teeth and mouths, which we thought was funny and we tried to outdo each other to see who had the blackest tongue. Then we were onto the large sugary rainbow balls, which lasted most of the afternoon. We didn't seem to mind each other's spit when we sucked and swapped them from mouth to mouth watching the colours of the round lolly change. At the same time, we watched the colour of the sky fade from bright to soft powdery-blue.

Later, when the westerly sun splintered the harsh light as it sat low in the sky, Jane and Johnno and I headed home and entered the front gate just as the sun slipped below the horizon. We walked down the sandy path towards the rear of the holiday house, as only visitors could use the front entrance. The dunny stood like a sentinel down the back. It was a scary place and everyone was wary of redback spiders biting their rear as they sat. The veranda had a single rope line to hang wet swimming costumes and towels. A bleached solid hardwood bench sat alongside the corrugated-iron rainwater tank near the back steps. The day's catch of fish flipped and flopped in a tub of salty water, ready for scaling, gutting and frying in dripping for dinner.

The weather was scorching during the day and balmy at night. All seemed surprisingly calm on the outside. However, the holiday week while our father was on leave from the hospital was fraught with undercurrents of anxiety. Our family felt like we were tiptoeing across a lawn full of bindi-eyes, careful not to upset the balance before Dad flew into a rage over seemingly nothing. Out came the 'no-noise' games, jigsaws, Monopoly, Squatter, draughts and Chinese checkers. We knew when to keep our voices to a whisper. After a family dinner of sorts, we kids escaped to the added-on covered veranda at the side of the house. There were fly screens all around to keep the mozzies out – no glazing at this stage – but maybe that was a good thing.

The nights were the worst. After a few drinks mixed with his medication, Dad would slowly build into a paranoid state, muttering responses to thoughts in his head, and ready to pounce if someone said the wrong thing. He would often lose control and rant and rave, usually when we were in bed.

One by one, we yawned the evening away and curled up in our bunks, though not always asleep. Sometimes we lay awake under the blankets, without a sound. I heard the thud of Johnno's balled fist into his mattress – over and over. Sleep eventually came for each, at different times of the night and early morning. Mum copped the worst of Dad's temper in the darkness. Nan and Pop kept their distance.

During the long summer days, we would sometimes catch the Southern Cross ferry past the Kincumber orphanage where a spooky old two-storeyed house held many children from 1887 to 1979. It was a boys only home until 1970, but we weren't to know that when Dad threatened to drop all of us off at the tidal wharf if we misbehaved.

At other times, it seemed as if a magic wand had been waved over the household when, armed with fishing rods and buckets, things seemed normal once more. Getting back into the groove of family life,

Dad would gather us together to take turns rowing the small wooden boat around the bays. We would come home laden with fish ready to fry on the barbecue. Once we even managed to hook a two-foot-long octopus which was lurking around the wharf's wooden struts. It squirted black ink to cloud the water, in an attempt to hide from predators like us. There was always a big batch of greasy chips to accompany the seafood, along with plenty of salt and lemons liberally squeezed over the lot. Dad would laugh and tell jokes. Mum smiled, while Nan and Pop temporarily lost their tense expressions and their wrinkles seemed to smooth over.

These were the good times. These were the stories I chose to tell my classmates, when back at school after the long Christmas break of 1963.

After the holiday up the coast, our family headed home. It didn't take much coercion to get Dad back to the hospital this time. His nerves were frazzled from the trip and he slumped in the front seat of the car while Mum drove him to the ward, along with a bag of freshly washed pyjamas, a few clothes and his cigarettes.

Dad's mood plummeted into a deep depression over the coming months, and shock treatment was deemed the order of the day for such patients. Luckily in his case, it worked. After a few treatments of ECT (electro-convulsive therapy), Dad had regained enough energy to get up to his usual antics of escaping whenever the opportunity arose. Nevertheless, his mood wasn't elevated enough to take away the despair, which frequently emanated from deep within. When he was down, he looked lost and hopeless, always wanting to be home. Dad said he was terrified of ECT. He often complained, 'They didn't give me enough bloody anaesthetic and I felt jolts go through me.' Mum, however ,maintained it was the only thing which worked when he was really unwell.

On more than one occasion, Dad decided it would be best for all the family if he were dead; a release for us to get on with our lives. Good idea, I thought at the time. His suicide attempts were recurrent and ineffectual – usually because someone found him in the nick of time with bloodied wrists, or an exhaust hose into the sealed car in the garage, or lying comatose next to bottles of tablets or poison. Dad never left a suicide note, and I imagine he was unable to even think of others when in those situations. Following each attempt, Dad was hospitalised until deemed recovered enough to be sent home to the family, until the next time. In many instances, the balance of his emotions tipped in the opposite direction, and his mood stepped up rung by rung, before soaring sky-high.

In the weeks and months leading up to each of Dad's admissions to psychiatric hospitals around the district, there was much distress within our family as his manic moods created chaos along with drinking, gambling, swearing abuse, crashing the car, breaking the furniture and the odd fire here and there from dropped lit cigarettes. Hours passed while he smoked and mumbled to himself when sitting at the head of the dining room table next to the sideboard, which held his overflowing ashtray. He interjected with outbursts of intermittent anger and fist-shaking towards someone who wasn't in the room. Dad said he heard voices in his head and imagined flashes before his face before shouting, 'Get out, get out!' At these times, Dad's pupils became dilated as he looked askance around the room. It was like living with a wild dog ready to attack.

The last straw before one admission was when our dad ran over and killed the neighbour's sausage dog, Banger. Our neighbours were rightfully upset, but thankfully understood it to be an accident – until Dad burst out laughing as he reversed the vehicle back from the squashed dog and called from the truck window, 'Sorry. That's a stupid name for a dog anyway.'

As expected, the neighbours rang the police. The mayhem in the street died down once our father had been carted off to hospital. The reprieve enabled us children to release pent-up frustrations with our home-grown game of Let's Kill Dad. We expressed our solutions, yet only within the confines of the family.

'I reckon if we put piranhas in his bath it will work.' I blurted out, proud of my answer to the 'Dad issue'.

'Well, I think piranhas beat my poison arrow idea,' Johnno said.

Jane, being a bit younger, couldn't really think of anything but tagged along with us, and Johnno would often pat his little sister on the head.

'I can never think of a good idea,' Jane snivelled.

'I win!' I shrieked with delight.

'Be careful what you wish for, kids,' Mum called from the kitchen.

5

Sea glass

During the mid-1960s as we were growing up, I became more aware of Dad's illness and the impact it had on our family and friends. It was something my siblings and I wanted to hide, fearing embarrassment and strange looks from neighbours and mates. None of us talked much about our feelings – it was all about Dad. We sapped up a lot of our emotional energy just coping with his unpredictability. He was becoming increasingly violent both physically and verbally, especially towards Mum when he was binge drinking. It was hard for us kids to intervene, but we tried, sometimes unable to reach our mother if she was locked in a room with Dad. Mum, always the peacemaker and our protector, shooed us away out of his reach.

This was happening around the time when our family had moved to a Californian-style brick bungalow in Lane Cove, where we spent the remainder of our childhood until we left home to go flatting with friends. These were the years Dad spent in Fraser House, due to our home being located in the catchment area for visits by follow-up groups from the therapeutic community.

Our new abode was also a bit closer to Nan and Pop's house, which was helpful for them when Dad was as an inpatient and Mum was expected to be a co-resident with him at the hospital. Therefore, during the weekdays, our grandparents regularly minded us in our house at Lane Cove, as we were getting older and they needed time to get us ready for school, and also be available to drop us to other activities in which we were involved, such as soccer and church fellowship.

Often on weekends, though, we would stay at Nan and Pop's place.

Whenever I arrived there, I would race down the darkened hallway past the cloudy mirror with bevelled edges, and stop at the old Margetson print hanging on the wall. It was named *The Sea Hath its Pearls*. I clearly recall the picture of a woman at the seaside in England looking at tiny shells in her palm. Sniffing hard, I could almost smell the sea and feel the sand between my toes. All my life I have done the same when at the beach, stooping to fossick through the sand for cowries and little treasures of opaque sea glass to add to my collection – each holding its own memory.

I remember playing in my grandparents' backyard. My sister Jane and I loved collecting eggs from the chook yard, where we would talk to our favourite feathered friends – brown Biddie and white Winnie. The wired area where the chooks cackled and clucked was adjacent to a dilapidated shed situated at the rear end of the yard.

Dark and dusty inside, the wooden structure was decorated with enough cobwebs to frighten the life out of me. The workbench was strewn with Pop's tools. Across the creaky floorboards in the far corner stood an old dentist chair, with ripped brown leather and swivel wheels. Constantly teased by Johnno, I was easily convinced it was an electric chair which had been used for killing people. I'd heard Mum talk to Nanna about the shock treatment my dad was having at the hospital, so from an early age I felt I had a good idea of how things worked. My heart sparked and hammered whenever I approached the shed. Sometimes Johnno waved an electric cord and plug, which sent me screaming to the back veranda and indoors for safety.

Often an egg or two would splat on the way. This of course, meant I was in trouble again from Nan for dropping them. Nan was aware of the teasing, so often let it pass as she got on with cooking cakes, pikelets and lemon butter. I was allowed to help mix the ingredients with a wooden spoon and soon forgot how terrified I was in the yard. My family loved Nan's sweet treats, though her bland boiled vegetables, sloppy steamed brains and tripe in white sauce were hard to digest. Everything seemed to have milk in it – for Pop's stomach ulcer.

The best meal of the week, though, was on Sunday. After church, Nan lit the oven with the already prepared roast potatoes, pumpkin and chicken. I tended to wolf down the gravy sodden vegetables and fiddle with the meat. Only a few hours before, while Nan was at the morning service, Pop would call us outdoors to choose a chook before he secured it to the pull-out ladder from under the shed. Wielding a sharpened tomahawk axe, in a flash he would chop off its head. Once untied, the bleeding bird ran headless around the backyard until it flopped in a heap. The chicken would then be plucked of its feathers, ready for Nan's roasting pan.

Another favourite game of Johnno's also took place at our grandparent's house. He was fascinated with Pop's rifle from World War I, and while there were no bullets in it, Pop allowed him to play with it whenever he liked, but only outside.

Petrified, my sister and I believed perhaps the gun did have a bullet. Even if it didn't, the way our brother hurled the heavy rifle with the bayonet attached, ready to stab oncoming soldiers in his war games, was enough to send us shrieking for help.

'Nan, Pop – he's going to stab us!'

'It's just a game,' Pop sighed, leaving Nan to tone down the play.

'Now keep it quiet, Johnno, and don't torment the girls. Pop's ulcer's giving him gyp again.'

Hunched forward, Pop would hold his stomach as he retreated into the formal lounge room, his sanctuary to read the newspaper with a cup of tea.

We kids were used to remaining silent when told to do so. Our mum, Grace, the dutiful daughter-in-law, made sure we behaved. She wasn't going to cop any criticism from a mother-in-law who thought no one was good enough for her son.

When it was time to leave, I would glance when passing the picture in the hallway, making a mental note to check my sea glass collection when I arrived home. Each piece varied in size, colour, texture and shape, yet all were smooth after tumbling and being washed back and forth in the waves, to finally settle at high tide somewhere amongst the shells and other debris. I loved the opacity, now cloudy like my memory. Moreover, each piece of glass had been something in a former life before its parent object was smashed or thrown, preceding the long journey to the seashore.

Sea Glass

a villanelle I wrote in 2016

Colours of the ocean, misty whites and hues of blue
Broken glass, on waves lured to a faraway land
Tossed and tumbled, into tiny treasures they renew

Where did you come from, the tide may give a clue
Irregular shapes, no two the same lie upon the sand
Colours of the ocean, misty whites and hues of blue

In a tidal rock pool, through rippled water I view
Tiny pieces awaiting to sift with my open hand
Tossed and tumbled, into tiny treasures they renew

Now opaque and smooth, it's why I search for you
Over time washed back and forth along the coastland
Colours of the ocean, misty whites and hues of blue

Once a useful item, into something more they grew
As fragments of the glass were swept by waves, and
Tossed and tumbled, into tiny treasures they renew

The sea I smell, lick the salt and wonder if you knew
Another memory now fills my pocket as I stand
Colours of the ocean, misty whites and hues of blue
Tossed and tumbled, into tiny treasures they renew.

6

Magical days

Throughout my childhood, many magical times were dotted amongst the demoralising and embarrassing moments, as I mixed with other kids from primary school. Even though Dad was ill, and bouncing back and forth from hospital, he did love his kids and tried his best to play Santa, Easter Bunny and the Tooth Fairy when at home.

Dad's fireman status elevated him to a hero in our eyes, when on Cracker Night he would keep a watchful eye on the bonfire. The logs and kindling had taken a couple of days to erect in the paddock opposite our house and Dad ensured that the fire didn't get out of control. Often, stray embers and sticks rolled from the perimeter base onto the grass. Our father quickly extinguished them before any tiny fingers or feet were burnt.

Always a bit of a rogue, Dad taught us how to cheat at poker, along with the skills required to baulk an opponent while playing chess. Whenever we were near water, we fished and learnt to become competent swimmers. In the surf, we were never afraid to swim out the back of the churned-up waves beyond the breakers. We knew how to get out of a riptide by floating with it, before edging parallel to the shore as it waned – a lesson which I adapted to other perilous situations in life. These were enchanted moments of childhood when Dad reminded me, as he often did, 'The best things in life are free.'

I often wondered what had happened to my father in those early days. He was well tanned, just over six foot tall, with shiny black hair to match his dark grey eyes. In his youth, he was a very good athlete and national sprint champion, as well as a first grade footy player and umpire. Later, when I read Dad's medical records, it was repeatedly commented upon how physically fit he was. Over many years, though, he did deteriorate and put on weight, due to his addictions to alcohol and barbiturates, along with side effects from medications.

Arguably, though, the most exciting thing to happen in my childhood was when I was ten.

'Do you get to keep the jelly beans?' my younger sister squealed.

Inwardly quivering, I dismissed her remark. I could hardly speak. This was my biggest day ever. The day I won the bike.

It began a few weeks before, in 1965 when we were living at Lane Cove. A typical Saturday started with the weekly grocery shop at the local Gumtrees supermarket. Perhaps this was one of the first supermarkets, and very small by comparison to those of today; more akin to an extra-large corner store. With three kids in tow, Mum and Dad led the expedition into the shop with the usual admonishments: 'Don't touch anything' and 'Stop fighting.' Of course, scrapping for a piece of the action was the usual state of play for me as a middle child. I was constantly harassed by my siblings and subsequently blamed for the arguments for being the loudest.

When we entered the shop, prominently placed on the front counter sat a large glass jar of jellybeans every colour of the rainbow. Next to the jar was an invitation to guess how many there were. The prize was a brand-new Malvern Star bike.

Could this be my big break? I wasn't going to let this opportunity go by, and neither were dozens of other local kids, who were also placing entries into the barrel. Accurately counting the jellybeans was impossible, which resulted in a rough guess. With my entry safely through the slot of the barrel and the shopping complete, we went home and soon forgot about the competition. The draw was weeks away, which felt like a year.

Oftentimes during those weeks, I had fleeting wishes and dreamt I could be the girl who won the bike. Reality quickly squashed my anticipation. Nothing lucky had ever happened to me, nor was likely to happen.

'Don't expect to win, and anyway at least you have a bike,' I was told.

True, I did have a bike, of sorts. I felt embarrassed riding mine among my friends with their shiny bikes and coloured handlebar tassels. I had a clapped-out old pale yellow hand-painted girl's bike. The paint looked like the same colour used in the lounge room at home, but thankfully it did cover the rust. My bike had no tyres. Instead it had metal wheel rims, which clanged and buckled as I pedalled. Occasionally my father or brother would wind some thick rope, or some sort of flat rubber, to soften the sound and the bumpy ride. Just keeping up was a challenge, yet I desperately wanted to be part of this new gang of kids in the suburb into which we had recently moved. The other girls didn't seem to mind, although I wasn't sure if they gossiped and sniggered when I wasn't around. I do recall odd stares from people as my bike rattled along.

The day arrived.

On my way to school, riding the clattering bike, an excited bunch of girlfriends rushed to me yelling, 'You won the bike, your name is in the shop window!'

This couldn't be true, not me, suddenly famous in our small community. It wasn't long before everyone knew. The onerous task of going to the supermarket window to check if it really was my name was ahead of me. Perhaps the girls were playing a trick on me, or maybe there was a mistake by the supermarket management in counting the jellybeans.

I knew I had to find out, so with fluttering trepidation in the half hour left before school, I rode with some others to the shop. Sure enough, the competition had been drawn and a sign in the window read, WINNER OF THE JELLYBEAN GUESSING COMPETITION, with my name beneath. There was a note below requesting the winner to see the store manager.

'Go on, go in.' My friends urgently pushed me through the door.

'Can I please see the manager?' I sheepishly asked.

'That's me,' he replied.

Identifying myself as the winner felt strange. I couldn't quite get used to the unexpected feeling of good fortune. My dilapidated tyreless bike always made me feel like a loser.

'Congratulations,' he said. 'You were the one who guessed closest to the correct number of jelly beans in the jar.'

There was probably a few hundred, maybe even close to a thousand. It seemed a lot anyway.

'Here's the glitch!' the manager said. Those three words nearly shattered me. 'You just have to answer one more question.'

HELP! I was about to wet my pants, cry or run from the shop. But the stakes were too high. I replied, 'What's that?'

He gave me a sneaky grin. 'What colour bike would you like?'

'Green, please.' I smiled as my dream came true.

The bike was delivered by a representative of Malvern Star, amid some fan fare a week or so later. It was a green, girl's bike with all the trimmings, including a bell, a wire basket and coloured plastic tassels from the handlebars. Best of all were the pump-up tyres, and even a pump to go with it. Perfect.

The answer to my sister's question was no, I didn't get to keep the jellybeans.

7

In the firing line

About the time I won my bike, the staff at the psychiatric ward of the general hospital realised Dad required a more contained environment. They soon transferred him to a new purpose-built psychiatric centre at North Ryde.

At the time, many old asylums around Sydney were slowly becoming more enlightened and opening their doors. However, this new centre was seen as very progressive and one of excellence. Its unique version of the 'therapeutic community' model, was different in some ways to others which were developing elsewhere around the world in the 1960s. When Dad was deemed to be less suicidal, he was considered for the Fraser House program. Unfortunately for my siblings and me, this meant Mum would be hospitalised as a resident partner. So, not only did we lose our dad, but also our mum. Which would be fine for most kids, I thought, but our parents didn't realise I was the one who got picked on by Nan, not big brother Johnno or sweet little Janey.

Years later in 2017, when I read Dad's old medical records, they stated that our whole family was admitted. Mum refused to let us sleep overnight, though, but we did attend groups and some other meetings when required. Given the options, I guess we were lucky to have our grandparents mind us at our home.

'If only I wasn't always piggy in the middle,' I thought. 'If Mum were here, she'd make sure we'd play fair and take turns.'

'Come on, Liz, we're ready,' Johnno called as he and Jane ran to the backyard.

It was inevitable in the 1960s, as a boy and the eldest, Johnno would lurch from playing with stick guns as cowboys and Indians, to Robin Hood and then to the battles of William Tell. The television show had given him ideas to modify his simple bow and arrow with a horizontal brace to fashion a crossbow of sorts. This created greater accuracy for shooting wooden arrows, carved sharp at the tip.

Johnno had been working on the new system all week after school with his grandfather. Now that Sunday had arrived he wanted to carry out a test run, ready to show off his skill to our father when he arrived home on day leave from Fraser House, along with Mum.

I crept outside following my brother and sister, trying to keep out of the way of Nanna who was preparing lunch for the family. This included cooking her son Rob's favourite, apple pie.

'No more apples, Johnno. I need enough for the pie,' Nan gently chided, with a grin on her face.

In the yard, Johnno organised the game. Now nearly eleven, I was placed in the garden with my back to the paling fence.

'Now keep still, Liz,' Johnno demanded. 'Don't move an inch – the arrow could kill you.'

Summoning all my courage, I tried to quell the thought of losing an eye, or worse. Paralysed with fear, I stood stiff and straight with my hands over my face. My knees felt like jelly.

Jane, the youngest, played the part of the ammunition soldier, carrying the bucket of apples.

Johnno placed the apple on my head and paced backward to the required firing distance. He loaded the wooden crossbow and pulled the string backwards until taut, releasing the first arrow, which flew to the left. It missed. My legs trembled, making me wobble.

'Stay still,' Johnno ordered.

Another and another, and then a few more arrows flew off course by a couple of inches. Johnno honed his aim as I flung my body sideways barely avoiding the point of the last arrow.

'That's it, no more moving – time for the blindfold.'

By this stage, I stood sweating under the darkness of the handkerchief tied around my face, knowing that the quickest way for the game to finish would be an arrow hitting its target.

'Good one. You got the apple at last,' Pop called from the window.

I heard my parents' car pull up. Flinging the blindfold away, I dashed sobbing into the arms of Mum, spluttering as I told the story of the latest game.

Mum hugged me tight while Dad, whose mood had lifted since we last saw him, sauntered vaingloriously through the house announcing his entry. He squeezed and kissed the family before striding straight to the backyard to assist Johnno.

'We need to refine this weapon, son, or we'll never beat the enemy.'

Father and son spent half an hour outside before Nan announced lunch was ready.

I noticed that our dad seemed really happy, laughing out loud and telling funny stories about the other patients at the hospital – although really some were quite sad. He seemed tense and his eyes darkened if interrupted while he was speaking, especially when I attempted to ask about someone who was sent to a locked ward. I then noticed Mum glance sideways at Nan, so didn't pursue the topic further.

The delicious smell of Nan's pie from the oven broke the tension.

As the dessert was placed on the table, Dad shouted to his mother. 'Whoopee. Hallelujah. Some decent food at last.'

Nan seemed pleased with herself. 'It's your favourite, lots of sugar and cinnamon in the apple pie.'

Dad gulped down his first slice and almost gagged on his mouthful as he spat into his plate. He thumped his fist on the table and began the tirade. 'Jesus Christ, CHOKOES, only fit for pigs, it's full of CHOKOES. Where's the bloody apple…'

'Don't blaspheme, Rob,' Nan interrupted.

'Well, where's the *damned* apple. I want my pie without the choko, makes me loco in the coco…nutty,' he clanged.*

---

* Changing or grouping/associating rhyming words spontaneously can be a

Nan replied meekly. 'It's okay, Rob, I just ran a bit short of apples because of Johnno's new crossbow.'

Dad banged the table. The plates jumped on the table and cutlery clattered onto the linoleum floor.

Jane was the first to cry, followed by me snuffling and wiping my forearm across my now dripping nose.

Pop intervened. 'Enough, son. Let it go,' he said as he left the table bent over with his hand on his stomach. 'I need to lie down. You're making my ulcer play up.'

Mum rose to clear the table.

Dad continued in his maniacal tone. 'Stop. No one's going anywhere, and quit that sniffing, Liz.'

Mum placed a hand on Dad's arm to calm him. 'Lunch is over.'

'Come on, Johnno, let's go out back for the archery contest.' Dad pushed his chair out and left the table. 'You too, Liz, we need you to stand still. You're our best target.' He laughed as if he had made a big joke, while each family member slunk off in different directions. 'Janey, hurry-up and get the bucket. Damn the chokoes – I want apples, get me apples...'

When the kerfuffle of the visit had settled, our parents returned once more to Fraser House. We three kids left at home were quiet – each subdued in our own way. I sensed there was a lot to talk about, but felt some things were best left unsaid. The afternoon slipped into dusk.

At dinnertime, Nan served up one of her more delicious meals of leftover rabbit pie and chips. The conversation petered out after we'd eaten extra generous bowls of tinned peaches and cream. Silently, Jane and Johnno and I drifted off to bed.

Late in the evening, the household was again tranquil. From my bedroom, I overheard snippets of the conversation as Nanna reminisced with Pop. Her marriage had been good: two happy children, a boy and a girl. 'And what a gorgeous boy he was,' Nan said, picturing her son's

---

symptom of a form of thought disturbance in psychosis for people with bipolar disorder or schizophrenia. (For more information see *DSM 5*, 2013.)

youth and vitality. 'Must have been the Black Irish on my side of the family that gave him those good looks.' She never had anything good to say about Fraser House, though. 'More like Calamity Cottage if you ask me. He's never been right since he went there.'

Our Nan wondered what happened and asked herself, 'Where did I go wrong? Was it my fault?' I can still recall the way she used to fiddle with her apron when deep in thought, as she watched the bent silhouette of our grandfather against the moonlight shuffling back indoors after his smoke.

'Come on, Eddie,' she said, 'time to get you into bed. The kids are nearly asleep and I've got to get their school things ready for the morning.'

Later, on reading Dad's medical records of those days, I discovered that Nan had, in due course, convinced herself that her son had nothing wrong with him, nor would he ever try to commit suicide, even though his attempts had been blatantly obvious.

The notes state,

> Rob's mother would not accept the fact that he was suicidal and… did all possible to avoid talking about it…she spoke only of superficial things in the meeting.

Mum also recollected later a doctor saying at the outset of Dad's illness that his mother had far too much attachment toward her son. For example in the early days in a private hospital after Dad had received his first ECT, he asked that only his wife see him. However, his mother had phoned reception beforehand and raced up to see him before Mum could get there, as she lived about ten minutes closer to the hospital and had a car.

Nan also mentioned over the years that her son had developed pink disease as a child. This was a common name given to acrodynia – a condition caused by heavy metals and specifically mercury, in the days when they were included in medicines and Calomel teething powder. Perhaps Nan later questioned her use of these everyday childhood medicines, though of course she wasn't to know the side effects at the time, and the medicines were taken off the market in the mid-1900s.

8

My birthday wish

Peering through the slats of the Venetian blinds on my bedroom window, I imagined the feathery streaks of clouds to be giant bird wings, stretching across the sky. Mesmerised, I was excited, joyful in fact. The day had started well. It was right in the middle of October – my birthday. Mum called me her spring lamb.

'Hurry up and get ready for school or I'll play merry hell with a big stick,' my grandmother Essie called from the kitchen doorway.

Jolted from my reverie, the day took on a routine like any other. *Uh-oh, in trouble again! Why does she always pick on me?*

I felt deserted and wished Mum could be home for my birthday. *Why did she have to go too, and leave me with them?*

After I'd packed my bag ready for school, my spirits lifted once more when I saw a parcel with my name on an attached card. I squealed with delight and unwrapped the crackly cellophane – just what I'd wanted: a new A-line style frock. Looking into the mirror, I held the musk-pink dress under my chin, delighted it didn't exaggerate my freckly skin. My dark brown straight hair had grown past my shoulders and my blue-green eyes reflected a faraway sadness back at me. I wanted to show Mum my dress straight away, though I'd have to wait until later.

'Thanks, Nan. I wondered whether you'd forgot. I love it.'

I went to give my grandfather a big hug as he sat in the corner groaning.

'Leave him be. His stomach's playing up again,' Nan warned. 'Now don't be late home. We're going to the hospital to have your cake with Mummy and Daddy.'

Shielding my face from Nan, I turned. I couldn't figure out what I felt – fear, anger, disappointment…crushed. Yes, that's what it was. Turning back to face Nan I said, 'Why do I have to have my birthday cake there?'

Nan sighed, weary from looking after three kids and a whining husband. 'Because your Mum and Dad love you and want to see you… and it's family group night.'

The hospital grounds were spacious and vacant, the ward airy and painted with a government-Issue pastel lemon. Mum met us at the ward door, and quickly ushered us out toward the shade of a eucalypt gum. Dad shuffled behind.

'Let's sit under here and have your cake. Go and have a look around, kids, while I have a quick chat to Nan and get the candles set up.'

I hated being excluded, so loitered nearby eavesdropping on the discreet conversation.

Mum spoke. 'I'm not letting the children stay the entire evening here. Can you mind them a bit longer?'

'Why can't you come home?' I pleaded to Mum.

Nan chided. 'Little pigs have got big ears.'

I skulked away, but soon returned when I saw the marauding sharks circling my cake. This had happened previously when other patients hung in the wings for a slice. Once our family had sung 'Happy Birthday' and I'd blown out my candles, all of them in one breath, I made a secret wish – the same one I would make for the rest of my life.

When the cake was cut – into as many pieces possible for a sponge with jam and melting cream – the other patients were given a slice. A young man came back for more.

'Piss off, Freddie,' Dad said in his drug-addled state.

I filled my parents in about school that day, where a few friends brought small presents. 'Can I have a birthday party next year? Pleeeease, Mum.'

'Of course you can…if things are okay at home. We'll wait and see.'

Wait and see…wait and see… How many times had I heard that over the years!

Nan cleaned up the picnic plates and napkins and watched her son Rob scuffle towards Fraser House. Surreptitiously, she wiped a single tear from her papery cheek with the back of her hand and gave my mum a quick hug.

Covering her mouth with her hand, Nan gave a short cough and spoke. 'I'll be waiting outside, kids. Come to the car park when the group therapy finishes.'

Like three little sheep, my brother Johnno, sister Jane and I followed Mum and Dad into the large lounge area of the ward. We positioned ourselves as close to our parents as possible on the vinyl chairs. The room soon filled with staff, other patients and relatives. About a hundred of them were cramped into the now-stuffy space. Some seemed strange, almost spaced-out. Others frightened me with their twitching and pacing. My body gave an involuntary shiver.

'Mum, why are some people still in their pyjamas?'

Mum whispered back. 'They're sick, not allowed clothes…shush.'

The doctor and the nurse began proceedings by asking people to introduce themselves and what they might like to discuss in the meeting.

By the time it was my turn to speak, something welled from within and all I could think of was 'It's not fair! It's my birthday and I want Mum to come home.'

My comment started a tirade. Some others began to blame family members for causing the patients' illness which had landed them in Fraser House.

'It's not all about one person,' the doctor said. 'We know that the whole family is sick, needs help – that's why we're in this therapeutic community.'

I cringed close to Mum. Jane and Johnno kept tight-lipped, eyes downcast.

Within the group, another patient screamed and hit her husband. He shoved her before nurses linked an arm on either side and led her away. The female nurse was clad in the distinctive blue uniform and the male dressed in grey trousers and a white shirt and tie. I noticed a few worried relatives glance toward the doorway, while others went on discussing things as if nothing had happened.

At one point, the group seemed to run out of steam. Yippee, I thought – we can go home now.

A forced silence followed, causing the discomfort and tension in the room to grow. Maybe the staff assumed this was a good idea… perhaps it would calm things down. No such luck. It did the opposite. The whirlwind of yelling and abuse took on a new direction.

'That fuckin' bitch stole my cigarettes. Give me one of yours…' demanded a man as he headed toward my dad and shoved him, also knocking me sideways.

Dad pushed the man back. 'Get away from me…and leave her alone.'

The male patient grinned and slunk off looking for another target.

Nothing was said by the staff. It seemed as if this was the usual turn of events in the group.

Until Mum spoke up. 'I think the children need to go now. They're too young to be involved here.'

When our mum attempted to leave with us, a nurse responded. 'I think the group needs to discuss this. Why do you think they should go?' She then directed her questioning to our father. 'Do you want them to go, Rob?'

'Let them go. They're tired,' he mumbled.

Dad's response didn't seem to suffice as an answer, and other group members began debating the point of whether we should stay or not. One woman got up and walked out, only to be drawn back inside. Another young man started calling my mum names. The staff seemed content to let the scene play out when my dad got up to walk out, only to be pushed back into the chair by the same man who had tried to cadge the cigarettes a few moments earlier. A scuffle took place. After trying to punch the man, our father was dragged off by a couple of hefty male nurses who loosened their neckties, while a young female nurse close behind jangled the medication room keys.

My mum knew what was happening and quickly shielded us towards the car park where Nanna was waiting. 'Take them home. It was a bit of a rough meeting…we'll talk tomorrow.' Mum quickly kissed us goodnight and rushed back inside.

Even strange goings-on seemed to become routine, which is what occurred over weeks and months when Dad was admitted as an inpatient to Fraser House, together with Mum.

I still couldn't understand why both parents had to be there, and I still didn't like being singled out by Nan whenever my siblings got up to mischief at home. Eventually, Dad was discharged, which meant Mum was also. Nan and Pop went home – about time!

It was great to have Mum back with us each night to help with homework, cook meals and read stories at bedtime. At home, Dad still voiced some crazy thoughts and his moods seemed to soar so high they got lost in the clouds at times. This entailed lots of mucking around and laughter – until he plummeted into nothingness.

It was less than a week after Dad had been discharged from Fraser House when I realised it wasn't over yet. Our joyful moments seemed so brittle, ready to be fractured in an instant.

'Quick, eat your dinner, kids, and clean up the lounge room. It looks like a pakapu ticket,' Mum said.

I usually laughed when Mum said those words. She often joked when I was little that my writing – scribble she called it – looked like a pakapu ticket. (This was a commonly used colloquial term derived from the indecipherable tickets used in the Chinese gambling game.) However, now Mum seemed to say it whenever things were messy. Tonight, though, she wasn't smiling.

'But we haven't finished our homework,' Johnno objected.

'There are visitors coming tonight, so hurry up,' Mum said as she cleared the dinner plates.

She and Rob had only been home from Fraser House a matter of days when the follow-up visits began once more.

I couldn't believe my eyes. Less than half an hour later, a rabble arrived in a van in the front of our house. Two nurses led the motley group, some still in pyjamas, into our lounge room. Plonking themselves down, the patients lit cigarettes, filling the small room with a grey mist as my mother served tea and cakes to stem their voracious appetites.

I wanted to scream, 'Get out, get out, this is our house!' I didn't, though, as Mum ushered the three of us to our bedrooms, along with a special treat, hoping to keep us occupied until the horde left – until the next time, and the time after that…

Recently I accessed my father's medical record of admissions. I pondered where my fury had come from about Fraser House and the big groups, until I read that this particular admission was preceded by Dad's suicide attempt – one of many, and the day before my birthday.

Dad had filled himself with medications, slashed his wrists and jumped into the Parramatta River. He was scooped out by the Water Police and taken to the local hospital to be stitched up before being transferred to the psychiatric centre. No wonder I was angry. It was yet another incident which had interrupted what was meant to be my special day.

I look back now and realise my father's despair at the time was all-consuming, to the point where he could not have even considered my birthday. He just wanted his life to end. In those days, Dad's illness was diagnosed as manic depressive psychosis (now bipolar disorder), along with psychotic depression and paranoia. Later, his mania became more florid and pronounced, but in those early years the despair Dad felt was insurmountable, dampening the joy in our lives as he sat and stared for hours into nothing.

I also recalled how panicky I was as a child in the Big Groups. Recently I read a paper explaining the system and group practices in Fraser House, which had come under criticism by some practitioners, as well as patients and relatives who had voiced their concerns regarding the groups.

The critics vividly describe to outsiders, their feelings of horror and helplessness when first exposed to the interrogation of verbal attack of a group of grossly disturbed people. Frantically, they look toward the staff for protection, but support is not forthcoming. The inescapable conclusion is reached: staff and (some) patients are united in their efforts to uncover innermost secrets and to probe sensitive emotional areas without remorse. (Clark, A.W. and N. Yeomans, 1965)

Notwithstanding this, senior staff had considered the involvement of children in Big Groups.

The policy of total family therapy has been further carried out by the increasing admission of whole family units, including young children… Admitting children to the Unit was undertaken with some trepidation. It was feared that what they would see and hear might harm them further. Many of them, however, were already exposed to gross pathological influences in their home and the risk was taken. While no obvious harm has resulted and much apparent benefit there is a need for caution and for a systematic and detailed study of the effects of the Unit on them. From the Unit's point of view their presence has been beneficial. Many patients who had previously displayed extreme forms of acting out, violence, abuse and the use of obscene language, modified their behaviour in the presence of children. (Clark, A.W. and N. Yeomans, 1965)

This was not the case from my memory. Often, discussions were heated and loud.

Mum, at age ninety-one, recalled times when the other residents would think and say in the groups that they thought she was 'too good' to have her kids stay overnight as residents. Mum's views were also backed up by our father who, even though he was unwell, did not want us to stay overnight. With the help of our grandparents to mind us, they made sure we never did.

9

Peaks and troughs

My family continued over the years to holiday at the beach house up the coast at Davistown. Along with my siblings, I spent many hours with Dad catching tiddlers and collecting green weed for bait. Oftentimes it was tricky navigating the three-man wooden rowboat around Brisbane Waters, which surrounded the beachside suburbs. There were fast-flowing currents between the small mangrove-edged islands and the strong possibility of a rip.

'Keep your eyes open and look for the patterns,' my father would say whenever the waters were treacherous. 'Keep your eyes open and you'll know where we are and what to do.'

I diligently looked for the patterns in the banded shades of water marking the depths. They graduated from sandy shallows to aqua ripples plunging into deep blue channels. We searched until we had arrived at the best fishing spots and threw out our hand lines baited with cockle meat we'd collected earlier at a sandy point on the shore where the currents met. Later in the afternoon, the atmosphere changed from fluffy white to streaky grey. The water was whipped up by the wind into salt spray. I felt the cool air of a storm approaching.

'Keep an eye on the sky,' I heard from the stern of the boat.

Floating cumulus clouds in the north were rushed along by angry black forms raging from the south. It was one of those days when the family arrived home just in time, before our little boat was swamped by the choppy swell.

On other days when the sun shone overhead, the shapes on the rock surfaces glimmered through the sea to reveal an interweaving web of sea life. I could clearly see to the bottom of the shallow water, ready to shout if we were in danger of going aground.

When Dad called, 'Watch out in case the ship hits the sand,' I giggled. I knew he really wanted to say, '…in case the shit hits the fan', but Mum always reprimanded him, 'Don't swear in front of the kids.'

When back on land at home, those balmy days gave way to darkness as the rhythmic waves of Dad's moods washed over him. Sometimes, he was on an even keel bouncing along in life with a soft steady rhythm. Other times, he'd ride the rogue wave so high he could hardly hold his suspicious and muddled thoughts together. Brash, loud and driving the car dangerously, he would laugh, literally, all the way to the bank, ready to back a winner as he gambled away our meagre family income. My siblings and I would keep out of the way and retreat to our rooms or friends' houses until the storm had passed.

Dad would subsequently plummet weeks later into the trough of the wave, in a slump of despair. While he suffered these deep depressions, the family felt a sense of relief – finally finding some peace following weeks of mayhem. Often during Dad's episodes, the local police cajoled and sometimes dragged him off to hospital. They knew him well, and we got to know them too.

On each visit to the hospital, Dad gave us the same advice. 'Keep your eyes open,' he'd mutter in a drug-addled state.

When our father's mood settled in the brief intervening periods, life was almost normal again. He went back to work as a fireman and all was going well. Stories of fighting blazes from the truck with thick hoses, especially during scorching summers, fascinated us. 'We knew to keep our eyes open,' he'd say, 'because most bushfires aren't started from lightning strikes.'

Dad was also wary of coincidences when it came to bushfires. 'Things just didn't add up that day,' he warned. 'I kept my eyes and ears open and watched the area for arsonists and firebugs,' he added, 'until it all came together and it was revealed the young lad who lived near the edge of the bushland was creeping about at night with matches and kero.'

From these stories, I learnt that some things were not always a freak accident or quirk of fate.

'Too many coincidences are more than just chance,' Dad said. 'They fit into a pattern. It's why you need to keep your eyes open – to find the truth.' He waggled his finger and nodded.

I yawned. My ability to stay focused and listen waned over time. I became blasé hearing his repetitions and paid little attention to the lessons and rants during my childhood. In fact, I'd heard him so many times, the hint of paranoia in my dad's voice became irritating. Best left alone, I thought. Ignoring the signs of his changing moods, I busied myself with my own life.

Nevertheless, those sayings have somehow stuck in my mind, ready to resurface when I could not see the logic in a particular situation. For instance, one evening in March 1966, when our mum was admitted alongside Dad in Fraser House, the group therapy session kicked off like any other. Dad was doped out on medication, and sat quietly with his head hanging down and eyes droopy. The evening Big Group followed the pattern of previous therapy sessions. Everyone was encouraged to speak, and if they didn't they were targeted, often by the staff. It was expected, by the mere fact of being patients in the hospital, that the inmates would be happy to expose their innermost feelings and bewilderment to a whole bunch of equally disturbed patients.

'How are you feeling today?' The doctor focused his question on my father.

'All right. Yeah, okay.'

Dad was pushed to explain why he'd tried to kill himself before his admission and if he really did feel okay. This went on and on until Dad struggled to get up and leave the room. Mum, who was also at the group session, began to follow. She was discouraged by staff and urged to sit, while they followed Dad. Apparently he was on close watch in case he made another suicide attempt.

Mum compliantly sat through the rest of the group and waited for his return. Alarms went off and a nurse ran to the phone. Another nurse then entered the group and whispered to the doctor, who quickened his pace in the direction of Dad's bedroom.

The story, my siblings and I found out later from Mum when she arrived home in the evening, was of Dad being harassed in the group. He had subsequently left the room to go to the toilet. He'd entered the toilet while the nurse waited outside. Foggy from the tablets, Dad said he slipped and fell with full force of his weight onto the toilet bowl. It smashed and a large chunk of broken porcelain caused a deep gash in his scrotum and cut through his urethra. The staff tried to quell the bleeding as they raced him to the surgical unit of the hospital.

Mum told us Dad had been transferred to the surgical unit on the campus, where he had undergone major abdominal surgery, after which he would spend some days recovering from the operation.

Well, that almost seemed normal to me – like other families whose parents had operations. It would be something to talk about at school, rather than the usual scenario of our dad being hauled away by police, and locked up in the loony bin to have shock treatment. Yes, I decided 'abdominal surgery' would be a good talking point.

I remembered Mum washing the pyjamas Dad had on the day he fell onto the toilet bowl. His clothes hung on the line, still slightly stained from blood. There was no cord in the pants. My mum found a spare one from an old pair and threaded it through. I also remember Nanna insisting in a hushed conversation with Mum how strange it seemed that her son would break a toilet just by slipping on it. What seemed odd to me, when I visited my father in the hospital at the time, was that a nurse constantly sat by his bed, even though he was getting up and around in the latter part of his stay. No other patients in the ward had a nurse with them all day and night.

When he was stable following the surgery, Dad was returned to Fraser House. The Big Group therapies were still held regularly. On his first day back, Dad was the entertainment, as our Mum would say. My mother cringed as she watched the eyes of the group shift toward her husband, before she heard the staff pursue him once more.

'Well now, you're back with us, Rob. Do you want to let the group know what happened? Let's discuss what *really* went on in that toilet.'

The events of that day finally added up. I realised years later it was merely another of our dad's up and down episodes, whereby Mum had tried to protect us from the craziness of the situations in which she found herself. She had always pointed out to us that Dad was 'sick', and his moods and thoughts were a result of his rattled nerves. She insisted our father was not a bad person and that he had always felt guilty after incidents when he'd hurt others or himself and let the family down.

Apparently, Dad had tried to injure himself with a sharp instrument, probably in response to bizarre thoughts affecting his behaviour. While in the small cubicle, he had fallen, which resulted in the toilet breakage and perhaps some further injury.

Dad's medical records from 1966 say he suffered from an acute paranoid reaction. Notes from the surgical unit explain that, while Dad said he slipped and fell on the edge of the toilet, the doctor saw otherwise and noted,

> I am not convinced of that…how this man could injure his urethra through the scrotum without further damage to his testicles beats me… The scrotal area…looks like a cut from a sharp instrument…ruptured urethra from fall/ self inflicted wound to the scrotum and urethra. The injuries required surgical repair via the abdomen.

Later in life, I understood the relationships between events as themes emerged – they were always there – though I didn't always see them when they occurred. I was older now and wandered the ward in Fraser House as I had as a child. His utterances were a reminder. 'Open your eyes and look for the patterns…then you'll know the truth.'

Dad and me, 1954.

Mum and me.

Back: Mum and Nanna. Front L to R: Jane, Johnno, Liz.

Dad, 1950s.

Dad in NSW Fire Brigade uniform.

Davistown holiday house, NSW Central Coast.

Dad and kids in rowboat on holiday, 1960s.

L to R: Johnno, Dad, Liz, 1960s.

Childhood home, Lane Cove.

L to R: Jane, Johnno, Liza, Manly Wharf, 1960s.

Dad's mother Essie.

Cousins from Mum's side. Liz is back 2nd left.

Cousins from Dad's side, 1970s.

Me and Mum, backyard at Lane Cove, 1970.

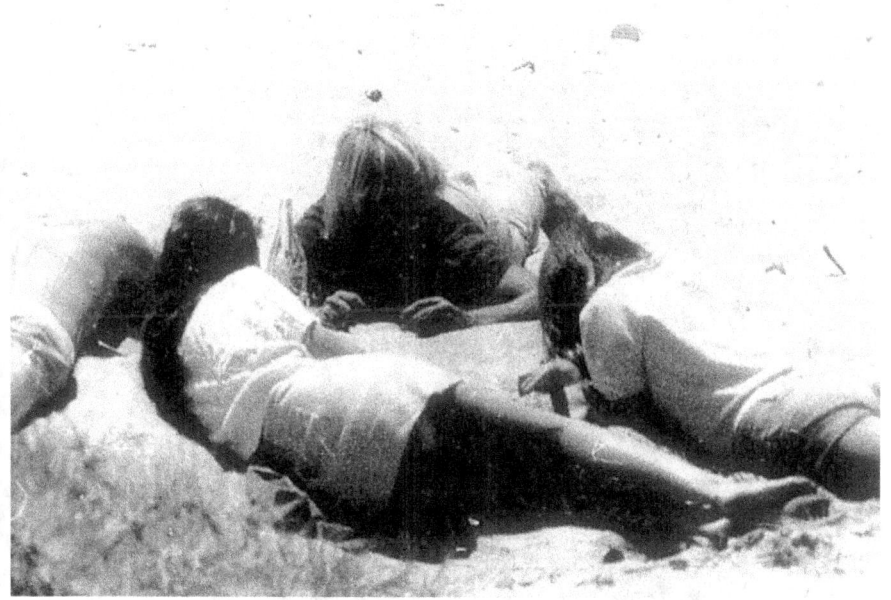

L to R: Liz, Dad, Jane, Christmas Day, 1970s.

Front: Liz and Jess, Aslings Beach, NSW South Coast, 1970.

Family brooch, circa mid-1800s.

Dad's bedside box and contents.

10

Fires

'Fireman, fireman, save my baby.' I recall Nan's words from when she told us the story of Dad's birth in 1928. It was her son Rob's entry into the world, and the maternity unit of the hospital was burning. Fortunately, all were saved as the firemen cleared the ward and the baby nursery. It was my dad's first whiff of smoke.

Over the years, the outskirts of Sydney and far reaches up the coast and inland toward the mountains blazed each summer. Often the haze partially obscured the blood-orange sun on the horizon. The smell of smoke in such skies became well known to Dad's senses, and it wasn't surprising when as a young man he joined the NSW Fire Brigade. This was much to his mother's delight as she proudly showed friends and family pictures of her son in his uniform with polished buttons and brass hat with the emblem of the brigade. Dad valued the camaraderie of the blokes he worked with. His strength and athleticism in early manhood made him suited to the job and well regarded among his peers.

Some firefighting tasks Dad encountered were worse than others. Mum knew the toll the fires were taking on her husband, because she had watched him fall apart after hours in harrowing bushfires. In one incident, the firefighters worked around the clock for nearly twenty-four hours straight at a major Sydney refinery. Oil drums hurtled into the air and exploded like bombs into flame. Dad was wrecked. It had been a bad night and there was a worse day to come.

I watched the television on such occasions, hoping for a glimpse of our father among the big red trucks and uniformed men.

Dad would arrive home exhausted, though too strung out to sleep. He would be awake and pacing for days, often leading to another admission to the psychiatric unit, with what is now called post-traumatic stress disorder. Other times, though, when the fires weren't so intense, he'd arrive home elated knowing all had gone well. After one particular event as a child, our family were bundled into the car and ventured to the blackened scene of a bushfire. Dad took us for rides on his back into the fire zone, once it was declared safe. The scent of wet, smoky wood and smouldering embers, covered with ash and twigs in the burnt-out space, was both fascinating and eerie.

'Why is it cold in here, Daddy?' I asked, expecting it to be hot.

'Don't know, sweetie. Just the way it is when the southerly buster comes through.'

Growing up, I learned to take note of the wind directions, ready to identify the familiar smell of smoke. This became imprinted in my brain, as well as in the minds of generations of our family. Memories of fires often resurfaced.

Later in the year of 1966, following Dad's abdominal operation – as the incident was thereafter referred to – he spent some time in Fraser House before discharge. Once home, the follow-up visits recommenced. The end of the year was approaching and I felt happy about leaving primary school, ready to begin afresh with a new bunch of friends. I looked forward to starting high school in the new year with a clean slate – without everyone knowing our family history.

Christmas Day began with the usual rush to open presents. I can't recall exactly what Santa had delivered. However, there were usually books, clothes and toys. We all remembered what Johnno got, though. He ripped open the wrapping and discovered, to his delight, the chemistry set which he'd longed for.

All together at last, and with no major drama, now that Dad had settled on his new medication, we took our places and sat at the laminex dining table. Before we ate, the bonbons were cracked open to reveal coloured crown-like hats, tiny plastic treasures and slips of paper with corny jokes. A favourite I still recall was 'Question: What do you get if a kangaroo mates with a sheep? Answer: A woolly jumper.'

'Ha ha,' Mum chuckled, moments before she abruptly ceased laughing. Her face changed. Sniffing hard, Mum rose from her chair. 'I can smell fire.'

'Sit down, Mum. Your food will get cold,' I said. We'd always had a traditional hot Christmas lunch, even when the temperature was over one hundred degrees Fahrenheit.

'I can definitely smell it,' she said.

'It's okay luv, probably bushfires out west,' Dad reassured.

Mum wasn't convinced. She left the table and sniffed her way to the scene unfolding at the side of the house.

'Fire! Come quick!'

Our family went into action. We were good at that – plenty of practice. I ran towards Mum, Dad grabbed the hose, Janie watched bewildered and Johnno stuffed a couple more gravy-coated roast potatoes into his mouth, while bolting to grab a bucket.

The smoke was billowing from Johnno's makeshift chemistry lab attached to the side of the closed-in back veranda.

Dad tried to quell the flames and then looked to Johnno. 'What chemicals were you using?'

Johnno reddened. 'Well, I mixed potassium and…' he replied, not fully remembering the sequence of events, as he had only just opened his new chemistry set. The many tiny beakers and pipettes were now broken and covered in soot. 'Do you think the shed will blow up, Dad?'

'Probably not, but we'll call the boys from the station, in case they need to check it out.' Dad soon had the fire tamed and continued to keep an eye on it while Johnno retrieved a few precious articles from his lab.

It was another humiliating moment for our family when the fire engine roared down our street. The nosy neighbours were out in full force once more, glaring at us. Mum off-handedly explained it was a minor mishap with the new chemistry set. When the crowd dawdled back to their houses, the looks they gave us said it all: that crazy family, always up to something.

With the crisis now abated, we finished our lunch and laughed about the chemistry set disaster.

Dad quoted again. 'You know, *the best things in life are free*. We're all okay and the house didn't burn down.' (Well, not that time.)

My brother, who had lost much of his prized Christmas present, didn't dare complain. After eating the plum pudding awash with custard, and counting up our sixpences, we took off into the street to play with others and compare our Christmas loot. We happily embellished the fire story for the neighbourhood kids.

Dad had a few more beers and soon fell asleep on the couch, while Mum sighed as she cleaned up the house, then the backyard, and picked her way through the damaged timbers for anything Johnno might find useful for his chemistry experiments.

During the following decade and a half, Mum put out many spot fires, as she called them, some with real flames, others a metaphor for a smouldering ember ready to ignite.

11

'The times they are a-changin' (Dylan, 1964)

'Quit fighting,' I screeched at my parents.

Stomping down the hallway, I entered my bedroom, which I shared with my younger sister. Through the doorway I looked to the window opposite. A sun ray refracted a rainbow through a tiny glass pyramid on the sill.

Four strides in, I bumped the end of my bed. 'Ouch.' I was always catching my little toe on the bedpost.

Flinging myself onto the mattress, I tried to calm down by gazing at the flickering light on my little glass treasures. Each sat on the thin ledge – a coloured fish, an open-winged bird, a bell and the pyramid prism. I was glad my bed was positioned under the window. After all, as the eldest girl, I deserved some privileges.

The window was an older sash style with two panes, one above the other. I imagined it as an escape hatch out of the turmoil of Dad's violence and drunken rages. The bottom pane was large enough to squeeze my body through, after a struggle. I'd attempted it once to check. Outside, there was a large drop to the ground, a problem easily fixed with a wooden fruit box to use as a step. The other confounding issue was the window had recently been painted. Much as I tried to pry the fly screen off, it was stuck, a bit like me. I needed to find the Stanley knife in the garage to slice through the paint – a task for another day.

I sighed. Even running away had its downside. Anyway, where would I go? I'd also have to bribe my younger sister to stop her blabbing to Mum and Dad.

The front door slammed, a signal Dad had taken off, at least for a while – a long while, I hoped. Maybe forever, but that was just wishful thinking.

I lay on my bed contemplating the next move. However, I eventually convinced myself things might improve. Settling down, I waited for my sister to return from her friend's place down the street.

With reddened eyes, Mum dawdled into my room. She hugged me. At times like this, my mouth dried up and no words came, so I stared out the window and said nothing. My escape could wait another day.

Jane came home half an hour later. The usual routine of dinner, bath and bed took over. We each retired to our own side of the room, though it wasn't long before she came across to me and we topped and tailed in my single bed. We'd done this for years. She loved to show me her dolls and teddies. We played for a while, except I really wasn't interested in those kid games any more.

When she fell asleep, I pulled the soft chenille bedspread with its waggly fringing up under my chin. Fidgeting with the well-worn fabric, I dreamed about my friend's sequined Indian bed cover. I wanted to scream to Mum, 'Can't you see it's time to change things around here?'

In 1967, I started secondary school at the local co-ed, Hunters Hill High, where I spent the next six years until the end of 1972.

During the next few years, Dad oscillated between inpatient treatment at Fraser House and other wards at the hospital, as well as community outpatient care, and evening groups and follow-up. Those times when our family was involved with Fraser House were memorable. During my childhood, still somewhat protected by the adults around me, I was too young to truly appreciate all that was going on. Dad's illness impacted our entire family, which took up most of my life apart from school, mixing with our close relatives and the neighbourhood kids. It was the period when I was maturing, on the cusp of adolescence. Confusing, yet enlightening years.

In adolescence, I was more aware of the wider world and continued, along with our family, to be involved in Dad's treatment via groups and meetings. Staff still saw some hope for him. It didn't seem that way to me, though. I had become somewhat desensitised to the madness. It was the only way to cope with constant rages and mutterings in response to his auditory and visual hallucinations.

I wanted to take flight from our crazy household, which was what I tried to do, while still living at home as the 1960s and 70s unfolded. I became involved with protest marches against the Vietnam War and South African apartheid, and for Women's Liberation and environmental issues, such as saving Kelly's Bush. This was a small piece of untamed bushland in the Sydney suburb of Hunters Hill and the planet's first Green Ban. Partying hard and taking drugs with friends and a few steady boyfriends, I found myself thrown into a somewhat crazy world.

Throughout my high school years, an escape route I discovered was a world of literature to complement readings on the school curricula. On my bookshelves I passed my fingers along the spines of Russian writers – Dostoyevsky, Solzhenitsyn, Tolstoy – and other books I preferred in those earlier teen years, such as Hesse, Hardy, Steinbeck, F. Scott Fitzgerald, Hemingway and of course the Bronte sisters. I plucked out *Wuthering Heights* and browsed through a few yellowed pages. It was, and still is, my all-time favourite. These books differed greatly from my earlier readings of my mother's eight-volume childhood set of *Anne of Green Gable*s. The main character, Anne Shirley, taught me to relish the tantalising taste of anticipation of future events, even if they didn't eventuate or ended in disappointment – a message I carried with me through my wild teenage years.

My world also opened up to a wider range of music: the first single 45rpm record I owned was 'Surfer Joe' with a flipside of 'Wipeout' by the Surfaris. I soon progressed to EPs and LPs of the Beach Boys, Dylan, the Doors, Joan Baez, Cream, Queen, more of the Beatles, Rolling Stones, Janis Joplin, the Who and many others. My brother and his friends, along with my girlfriends, turned up the music and played these records over and over as we sang and practised the latest dancing – the Twist, the Stomp and the Swim.

One good thing which happened at the end of 1967, which I had forgotten, and only read recently in Dad's medical records was

> Wife requests no more home follow-up groups at present, as they are attending weekly groups.

I wonder why? Perhaps the blaring records we played of Hendrix and the Stones, which reverberated through our house during the last follow-up visit, had worked.

12

Teenage runaways

Serendipity struck when I was in high school and met someone who would become my lifelong friend. Jess enrolled at our school in the last term of our first year. We were both only twelve and would become teenagers by the end of the year. She lived locally and had begun her secondary schooling at a private girls college, following in the footsteps of her sisters, who were a year or so older. Unfortunately they were asked to leave for various misdemeanours and subsequently were sent to our local co-ed high. So I guess I was in luck when Jess insisted she also leave where she was currently enrolled to be with her big sisters.

Jess also experienced mental health problems within her family, and she was the only other friend I'd met who seemed to endure chaotic crazy times. We stuck together in our silence, knowing that when things became intolerable in our households, we could bolt to the other's. Finally, I had an escape hatch. We have remained best friends for over fifty years, and have run away together – twice.

The first time we ran away was a couple of weeks before our School Certificate exams in 1970. I was sixteen. I'm not sure what prompted us to flee, maybe exam pressure, turmoil at home or the antics of my current boyfriend, who was a bit strange – he smoked too much dope and thought he was a Viking when tripping on acid/LSD.

Plotting our escape, Jess and I offered a lame excuse to one of the teachers and left school early one afternoon. Briefly, we stopped in at each of our houses to pack a handful of basic things and jumped on the 254 government bus to the city. We alighted near Wynyard Station and caught the next train to Central. To avoid anyone recognising us, we needed to disguise ourselves. In the ladies toilets, we changed clothes in separate cubicles, rearranged our hair, donned a scarf and piled on lots of make-up to give the impression of being older.

Walking into the country train platforms area, we examined the huge vertical boards for the timetable to the Riverina. The plan was to go fruit picking and travel around living on a meagre income and going up 'easy street'.

With shaking knees and trembling hands, I asked the booth officer for two tickets and handed over the money we'd saved. We laughed out loud, 'We're off to the Riverina.'

Making our way to the platform, we quietened down as we scanned the area for truancy officers. We continued to try and look inconspicuous with our bright red lipstick, sunglasses and carry bags. In hindsight, I can see this was a bit of a giveaway.

'What do you two think you're up to?' a voice boomed from behind.

We turned to find a policeman beaming down on our now pale faces. I'm not sure who tipped him off – probably the ticket booth man.

Within seconds, another police officer arrived, a woman this time. Bundled into the police car, we were taken back to Jess's house. Her parents and big sisters were waiting. To my dismay, my parents were also there, after having been summoned by the police. I later discovered that, they had been alerted to the runaway incident by my boyfriend, whom I'd let in on our secret plan just in case I decided to write to him once we were settled.

It was the ultimate betrayal, so that was the end of him. Following a big pow-wow of rage, tears, apologies and promises not to do it again, some rules were laid down for the next couple of weeks before the exams. However, for me there was worse to come.

The rules were what hurt the most. Jess and I were banned from seeing each other, except during our time at school, until after the exams. We were also barred from phone calls. Usually we talked all day at school and afterwards at the Aristocrat café – the Arrow. At the end of each school day, we liked to follow up with any new gossip or schemes each evening by phone. The no-phone rule was almost impossible to adhere to, so it wasn't long before we broke it whenever we could take a chance.

I was caught once making a hushed phone call early in the evening, just as Dad was entering the lounge room to turn on the evening news. I was trapped, as the bakelite phone was anchored to a wall in a cubbyhole around the back of the door. Enraged, he swore abuse before kicking me in the corner, resulting in a couple of bruises. Defeated, I cowered like a quivering rabbit whose burrow was about to be closed off with the force of another footfall. When Mum tried to intervene, I seized the opportunity, banged down the receiver and shoved my way past Dad. I scurried to my bedroom, slammed the door, fell onto my bed and cried myself to sleep, which wasn't unusual in those days.

Once the School Certificate exams were over, our household calmed down a bit.

However, my father forced me to get a job straight away. 'School's finished and you're not going back.' He thumped the table.

I argued against the decision. However, in the end didn't feel I had much choice. I found a full-time clerical office job at North Sydney which required commuting by bus. The job wasn't too bad to begin with, so easy in fact that I'd mastered everything I was supposed to do in the first week. In the weeks thereafter, I was bored to death, imagining working forever in an office. I decided never to learn to type, fearing it would restrict my life to office work. My brain screamed for something different.

The day the exam results were published, my shaky hands opened the newspaper with some trepidation. After all the hurdy-gurdy of the past months, I really wasn't sure how well I'd performed.

I ran my finger down the page until I reached my name. Against each subject sat the letter 'A'. Six As! Top marks. I shrieked around our house before grabbing the phone to see how Jess had fared with her results. I held back a little, just in case she hadn't achieved the marks she wanted. Hooray, Jess also got six As. Phew!

I was desperate to go back to school to complete my final two years and sit the Higher School Certificate, HSC. With such a good result, I believed I had a point in favour to push my case. Mum also tried to convince Dad to let me return; yet he steadfastly held his position.

No congratulations were in order when Dad replied. 'She doesn't bloody need an education. Girls just get married.'

A bit rich, if you ask me, I thought, given our father had been sick and mad for most of his married life with only intermittent employment. Meanwhile, Mum worked full-time as a secretary/assistant to the national finance manager of a large Australian company, just to keep the bills paid. And to top it off, whatever Dad earned was usually blown on booze, smokes, horse races or pokies. I recall even as a young child worrying after overhearing the arguments our parents had about money and the inability to pay the bills, especially the Grace Brothers account, where Mum could put food on credit when the cash was low after Dad's gambling losses. I would sprint home from school after hearing these fights wondering if Mum and Dad had been taken to jail for not paying up. Hence, when I was old enough, when I turned fourteen (I was tall and lied about my age), I secured a job cleaning in a large general hospital after school two days a week, and squirrelled away my wages in case the money was needed to pay bills.

Weeks passed and nothing was changing for me after the School Certificate. Reluctantly, I trudged each morning to my office job. Fellow school friends were celebrating, holidaying and perhaps getting part-time jobs over the long break until their final senior years started the following year.

Towards the end of the year, the office I worked at shut-down for a week or so over the Christmas period. I couldn't wait to call Jess when it was confirmed how many days I would have off. I was ready to escape the city.

'Great. Let's go on a holiday to Eden,' she said.

It didn't take us long to prepare for the trip and we would stay with Jess's grandparents, who lived on Twofold Bay, in a quaint weatherboard house near the main wharf of the south coast fishing village. I'd earned enough for the train fare to Nowra and had some spending money. We had a joyous few days with her grandparents, walking, swimming, fishing and relaxing. She and I both had a brief holiday romance with a couple of local boys and spent each day at Aslings beach, and at their place most evenings. Later, we headed back to the grandparents' house before midnight and after they had gone to bed. I think they were a bit deaf as they never seemed to hear us scramble up the gravel path.

One particular night, a few days before our holiday was due to end, for some reason – and I can't remember why – this was to be the second time we ran away together.

Something transpired and passed between us that night which words can't describe. It was a compelling need to flee – a feeling which surfaces in me every now and then but never leaves me.

The tide was high as it lapped the wharf and a pearl moon lit the sky. The room where we slept was hot and stuffy, even though the fuel stove was no longer burning. Tossing and turning, we couldn't settle with our sunburnt skin scratchy on the sheets.

About three in the morning I whispered, 'Are you awake?'

'Yes, let's get out of here.'

Within minutes, we'd stuffed our few belongings, towel, bikini and a couple of T-shirts and shorts, into our striped fabric beach bags. Carefully we lifted the squeaky window, fingers crossed the grandparents wouldn't wake. Climbing out, we stepped onto dry bushes, where brittle twigs scrunched underfoot.

'Hurry up,' Jess hissed.

Leaving the window ajar, we snuck far away from the house before we spoke again. We attempted to hatch a plan – which was a bit difficult at three a.m. Our best option was to wait for the first bus out to Nowra train station, which went at about six a.m. for commuters.

Dozing at the bus stop, we stirred at first light when others arrived. Minutes before the bus was scheduled to depart we phoned both sets of parents. Jess asked her parents to ring her grandparents. We hadn't really thought this escapade through. Nonetheless, we didn't want the grandparents frantically thinking we'd been abducted through the open window when they woke to an empty house.

Finally we took our seats on the bus to freedom. Freedom from where I can't explain, because we were already on holiday and were now heading home, where we wanted to escape from in the first place. At Nowra, we transferred on to the train to Sydney. When safely back in the city and inside our houses, once again we had a family meeting about the incident. This time we were a bit older – albeit only a couple of months – and didn't feel the need to explain ourselves, so we sat tight-lipped until we were left alone.

Recently, Jess dug out her old photos and found one of us at the beach with the two boys, all of us photographed with our backs in the foreground lying on the sand talking to each other.

A thought came to me and I asked. 'Who took the photo?'

'Don't know.'

To this day neither of us can answer the question, though we still cherish the photo and chuckle at our memories of climbing out the window.

Decades later, I recalled my teenage runaway instances. I pondered all those times Dad had absconded, gone AWOL or failed to return from granted hospital leave. His medical records are littered with 'escapes', as he called them. This was possibly one of the reasons he was such a revolving-door patient, since he never stayed long enough to completely settle with prescribed treatments.

Wondering why the compulsion to flee still sat at the back of my mind, even though I no longer acted upon the urges, I mused, 'Is a runaway the same as an escapee?'

I needed to decipher what made me go back, and what kept me there. I realised sometimes people do run away and never return, yet more often the fact is they go back, over and over. Therefore, instead of thinking about what made me escape, it seemed just as important to turn it around and figure out what made me stay or want to return. Fear, familiarity, family – love.

13

'School's out for summer' (Alice Cooper, 1972)

1971. I did go back to school, but not without a fight.

I was still working at my tedious job after New Year when everyone else was enjoying the last weeks of the long summer break. I used to catch a bus home, which detoured via Jess's house. This was where I would break my journey and chat with her for a couple of hours. We still talked about me going back to school and she gave me tips to try and persuade Dad to change his mind. During the evenings at home, I was exhausted listening to Dad's utterances, where fantasy and reality concertinaed together in a single sentence. At the same time, I tried to home in on Dad's patches of lucidity, ready to convince him to allow me to finish my education. Unfortunately, I often floundered for words as I attempted to make him understand the enormity of my needs.

Jess and I also spent some weekends at the beach, where in my gloom I flopped on the sand like a tired dog. I dreamt of blotting out my past and changing my life, yet felt hopeless pondering how I could make it happen. Over time, I came to realise my chaotic childhood living alongside Dad's illness had caused me to slowly build a carapace around myself. This strong shell was a refuge into which I could retreat when the storms raged around me and the emotional battering was too close to bear. It's what they now call 'resilience'.

The crisis point was reached when the school year began. I continued to be employed full-time and kept up appearances of normality at work, even though my mind was elsewhere. Time was running out and I wasn't going to give up yet. Emboldened, I pestered

Dad every minute whenever I felt he was receptive to hearing my plea. Mum and my brother Johnno, who was then starting uni, also helped. In the end, my bloody-mindedness enabled me to wear Dad down – or maybe it was his illness and he just gave in. He plunged soon after into another major depressive episode – not my fault, though, I told myself; it would have happened anyway.

On the Sunday night when I finally got the go-ahead to return to school, my first action was to telephone Jess. It was a short call, and when I heard her voice quaver, my eyes welled up. I asked her to let teachers know the next day that I would be coming back, though not sure when, because I needed to give notice at my job on Monday morning.

After handing in my intention to quit, I worked for two more weeks before triumphantly walking back through the school gate. It was where I needed to be.

The final two high school years were some of the best years of my life. I grew away from my dizzy early teen years, and enjoyed studying, going out with friends to parties, and heady days of rock concerts, such as seeing Led Zeppelin in 1971, where I swayed on my boyfriend's shoulders at the front of the stage, within a few metres of Robert Plant, as he boomed out the 'Immigrant Song':

> We come from the land of the ice and snow
> From the midnight sun, where the hot springs flow…

I felt the lure to escape to a faraway land – though didn't act upon it.

Life at home was more of the same. At the beginning of my final school years, Dad's moods see-sawed. Unfortunately, he rarely stayed long enough in hospital to be treated adequately, yet was often viewed as sane enough to stay out of the way of police, until his psychosis or disturbing behaviours escalated to a crisis, whereupon he was certified under the Act.

At least Dad received some good community care when he was at home. Towards the end of the year, he was drinking heavily, not coping and severely depressed. It was to be his last admission to Fraser House, which closed around that time, being integrated into other admission wards as the system changed with more community care and crisis intervention. During this admission he had, along with medication, another course of ECT. As per his usual practice, after a few ECTs Dad went on weekend leave and refused to return, so again was referred back to the community centre.

We strove to be an everyday family as we brought friends home to play records, and smoke and drink on our back veranda. Dad took up his usual position next to the sideboard in the dining room with his smokes and a bottle of beer. He shuffled his feet back and forth wearing the carpet threadbare. Often, when he was well, he'd come and join us, tell jokes, talk politics and debate religion while banging on about the Catholics persecuting him – possibly due to our Irish surname and the local priest dropping in from time to time unannounced. I think our friends knew Dad wasn't quite all there, but didn't mind him sitting happily alongside them.

In 1972, my Higher School Certificate year, Dad's moods were all over the place. Towards the middle of the year, Mum's job often required her to work back to get the company's financial figures ready for tax time. On those days, she was home late.

Coinciding with these times, Dad's mood spiralled up again. He'd habitually stare at the Namatjira print of the Kimberley Ranges, which hung above our fireplace, as he fiddled with two decorated boomerangs sitting on the shelf near the picture. He was inspired by how Aboriginal people survived in the outback and other remote areas. Often Dad would bring home a wetted hessian sugar bag full of sandstone chunks laden with Sydney rock oysters, ready to shuck and eat straight from the shell. He also imagined he could live off the land in our suburban Lane Cove home. This led him to attempt to make dinner while Mum was still at work. We arrived home to see garden snails hanging from the clothesline in the backyard. Each slimy grey slug had a fishing line hooked into its flesh – waiting for their shells to drop off. He served them fried in butter with what he beieved to be witchetty grubs from the rich soil at the front of our house. To complete a well-rounded meal, Dad boiled spinach: not the tasty green leaves, but only the white stalks chopped up – the leaves were discarded in the bin. After meals like these, it was hard to pretend we were a normal family, so I avoided conversations at school about what we had for dinner. Stalks, snails and witchety grubs didn't sound appetising. If pressed, my standard answer was 'meat and vegies'.

During the second half of my HSC year, Dad was sliding down again. He was sent to an admission ward of the psychiatric centre where he was diagnosed with the usual: MDP – depressive phase. However, now barbiturate addiction and asthenic type personality disorder was also added. He was treated for five weeks and sent home on trial leave, where he managed for a couple more months until he made another potentially lethal suicide attempt.

After studying late one night, I closed my eyes as daylight dawned, hoping to savour another few precious minutes, when a siren wailed down our street. After being found by my brother, Dad was hurried to the local emergency department with slashed wrists and bloodied arms, topped off with an overdose of weed poison. Mum was contacted at work while Dad was getting stabilised. Once medically cleared, he was transferred under the Mental Health Act to a locked ward of the psychiatric centre.

After spending several weeks in a secure ward, he was relocated to a more open environment. When he improved, Dad was given leave to work at a hostel and trial some weekends at home. This admission, I noted from his medical records, was for the duration of five months. It was probably the first time in years he had stayed long enough to receive some lasting treatments. Dad's records state he was angry and violent when on leave at home. He also complained, 'My wife wears the pants…' Well, someone had to feed us and keep a roof over our heads!

Dad became very lethargic, gained weight, and suffered low libido and impotency from the tablets, which contributed to his irrational, psychotic and insanely jealous accusatory behaviour towards Mum. The doctor also discovered, through blood tests, that Dad had hypothyroidism, which was subsequently treated. Mum latched onto this organic finding, hoping the drugs would improve her husband. A treatable illness at last! Nevertheless, nothing much changed. One good thing, however, which did result from the long admission was that the staff finally made him take his medication via a long-acting intramuscular antipsychotic. The drug, fluphenazine decanoate (Modecate), is no longer used, due to the development of newer drugs with fewer side effects. Nonetheless, at the time it did manage to keep Dad stable and out of hospital for long periods following his discharge, when combined with regular injections and follow-up in the community.

Of course, during this year, I was trying to study and do the required assignments for the Higher School Certificate, while Dad was raving and banging things around the house. Even when he was admitted, we kids were also expected to visit the hospital regularly.

I couldn't wait for the exams to be over, imagining partying late with my friends into the night singing, 'School's Out for Summer'.

In October, the day finally arrived for the exams to begin. I set off for my first English paper, found my desk, arranged my pens and told myself to focus. I forced myself to forget the thuds and sounds of breaking glass the night before and block out the smell of the beer-sodden carpet. I wanted to wipe the image of Mum dabbing make-up on her bruises as she readied herself for work, before facing another day.

14

Moving on

Kookaburras cackled as they called for the rains to come. It was the day of my maternal great-grandmother's funeral. My cousins and I called her Big Fat Nanna, to distinguish her from her daughter, our grandmother. It was 1972 and she was ninety-two. It had been nearly two hundred years since Mum's side of the family arrived as convicts on the Second Fleet in 1792 aboard the ship *Indispensible*. Nanna was a vital part of our lives and would have laughed along with the kookas, welcoming any drop of rain on the parched outback plains where she lived most of her early years.

Nanna had husbands aplenty, who all died. She didn't kill them – just outlived them. In her last couple of decades, Nanna resided in Sydney, though before that lived in Coonamble, country NSW, and surrounding areas near the Bogan River. She could spin a good yarn and told stories of her time as a governess on an outback station where she met the legendary Clancy. She told me of the mischief which she and other station girls got up to towards the 'haughty' poet Banjo Paterson, who came to the property to pick up his supplies. One of their pranks involved smearing honey on his saddle – you can imagine the flies following him on his outbound ride.

I visited Nanna quite a bit in the last couple of years before she died, and this is what she said to me: 'Life passes too quickly, especially those bits that make it worth living.'

Nanna reminisced of the days and nights when she nursed an old indigenous man who lived along the Bogan River area, until he died.

This must have had an impact on her, as in her later years before her own death she told me, 'Every day since I turned seventy, my three score years and ten, I counted those days as a bonus. Sometimes at night that old blackfella would come to my door, to take me away from this life. I would whisper, I'm not ready yet, and he would slowly fade away... Each day gave me a little more time.'

I guess when she did finally go, he'd said, 'Time's up.'

Not long after Big Fat Nanna's death, Mum handed me a brooch. I had seen it worn over the years in old sepia and black and white photos, pinned proudly on previous grandmothers. She and her mother had received it many years before from their own mothers and so it continued a journey of being handed down at some arbitrary elected point in time, by the eldest girl of the eldest girl, for generations. Luckily, we do tend to breed females in our family. Thus far, it has lasted in the chain of descent since my great-great-grandfather acquired the gold nugget on his commutes as the first Cobb & Co. coach driver from Parkes to Peak Hill during the gold rush days.

In a worn-out velvet-lined box, the brooch sits snug. It is old and tarnished set in a pinky gold and contains a lock of hair curled in the back compartment, and adorned with a single emerald and diamond on the front. It's not big by today's flashy standards, but it remains precious to us. As a symbol of family unity, the brooch holds the memories and stories of past lives.

Nanna was also a great one for quotes. After she died, I was given her old recipe collection. It is kept in a lined exercise book, now tattered and falling apart. At the end of each page of faded blue-inked beautifully scripted recipes, she had written a quote or a favourite saying. On the first page, following the recipes for picked cucumbers, orange jam and jellies, it reads. 'The sweets of life are not found in family jars.'

I missed her when she'd gone. As her earthly life ended, my life was beginning. At age eighteen, I had imbibed Nanna's lessons, ready to get out of the family home and forge my own path in life.

After the HSC exams, I didn't get a job straight away. Bag packed, along with dozens of other kids, I headed on a road trip up the north coast. We swam, relaxed and laughed during those few weeks while waiting for our results to decide what would come next. At the end of the long summer holiday, I returned home with a broken arm after being bucked off a horse and concussed. My bank account, in which I'd accumulated a tiny amount from working after school since I was fourteen, was also broke. I realised living an independent life would be harder than I thought – a job was essential if I wanted to move out of home.

Arriving inside our front door, nothing had changed. Mum was at work and Dad sat smoking, mumbling and drinking. In case he hadn't noticed the plaster cast, I told him the story of my broken arm.

'Never mind,' Dad said. His eyes flicked to each ceiling corner looking for things not there, before grumbling incomprehensible words.

At this stage, I was feeling somewhat indifferent toward Dad's madness. I headed to my room, unpacked and tried to figure out my next steps. It didn't take me long to reach the conclusion I couldn't go straight to university, as I needed to support myself – my uni days would come later. A couple of friends were doing nursing, so I followed them and enrolled in a general nurse training course, which at that time supplied board, food and lodging within the hospital, and a meagre salary. It was enough to enable me to live independently, at least for a while.

The 1970s was the decade in which I felt I finally won some control over my own destiny. I'd settled down from my rebellious teens and worked and studied. My fiancé and I were married and we moved into our own home. As well, my brother and sister had married and left home. Mum, now with an empty nest, even though we visited often, was left exposed to Dad's mood changes and vitriolic rages. During the 70s, Dad was often brought into an admission ward at the local psychiatric hospital, accompanied by the police. He was deemed either unable to care for himself, or not under proper care and control, so met the criteria for involuntary admission on a Schedule II under the Mental Health Act.

I recall an incident when at home visiting my parents. Dad had been up all night disturbing the neighbours, playing loud music, singing, swearing at voices only he could hear, before ringing the fire brigade and the church minister at all hours. He swore at me when I tried to intervene and then hit me. The police were ultimately called with Mum screaming, 'I can't take any more.' During this admission, he was diagnosed with chronic schizophrenia, which added to the list of other diagnoses. However, the discharge summary on Dad's records state, 'Opinion was divided as to whether this man was schizophrenic or was a decompensating personality disorder with depressive features.'

Even so, Mum did stick around a bit longer, though she would eventually move out in the latter half of 1978. I guess she had always loved Dad and compelled herself to see through his illness to the man she'd married.

Earlier that decade, Dad's father died, which precipitated a depressed phase in my father's mood, requiring another extended admission. Dad's medical records say he believed his father had died of 'sand pollution and poor food while serving in the Middle East in World War I'. I'm not sure what he meant by sand pollution. Perhaps, as my grandfather was a Light Horseman, he had suffered lung damage during sandstorms and battles. Pop certainly had a stomach ulcer, though, and never stopped whingeing to my grandmother when his ulcer was giving him gyp.

Soon after Pop's death, Dad's mood cycled up once more to the point where he became paranoid regarding Mum, saying she was trying to 'brainwash' him. The voices and delusions in Dad's mind often led to aggression. He believed 'the world would be destroyed by enzymes and that his family were conspiring against him' (from record). His erratic behaviour remained unchecked by any of us kids, as we weren't living at home, although at the time I lived the closest so was often called upon. However, when things escalated out of control, somehow Mum or the neighbours made sure he was admitted, usually involuntarily. Fraser House had closed some years earlier, so Dad was sent to locked wards before granted leave once he had settled down. This was beneficial. At least it was getting him to adhere to treatment for an extended period of time and take his medication. Nevertheless, the progression of his illness seemed unrelenting and intractable.

During one particular admission, Dad was allowed weekend leave for my wedding. I recall the lead-up, and the day itself, as a time fraught with heightened anxiety. Conditioned over the years to disarray, my default position was one of wariness. I was fidgety and my heart was jumpy, wondering what havoc would unfold on my special day. Walking down the aisle, accompanied by my shambling father, I saw my whole life pass before me, a blurred vision through my tulle veil. Forcing a smile, I looked to the gathered friends and family. We had arranged a lunchtime wedding in the hope Dad would remain sober enough to see the ceremony and reception through before he tipped over the edge again. Hence, I couldn't wait for the lunch and speeches to finish. Late afternoon, I sighed with relief driving off with my husband.

While I was enjoying a break on my honeymoon up the north coast, Mum was left with the task of getting Dad back to the ward the following day. Recently I read in Dad's medical file some notes of my wedding weekend in 1975, which state that when Dad returned from weekend leave he was in a miserable, almost mute state. He told the staff his depression was 'because of let down after the wedding'. He then remained in hospital receiving ECT and other treatments for another three months. It was to be his last admission to the psychiatric centre at North Ryde. Following discharge, community care kept him out for a while, and thereafter he was admitted to the older-style Gladesville hospital on the banks of the Parramatta River. While there, Dad was seen by the magistrate and made a 'Temporary Patient' under the Act, which enabled the staff to keep him for longer periods, with the added ability to grant trial leave when he was well enough.

In 1978 Dad's mother died. She was in her eighties. Nanna had been senile for a year or so before her death, and we all visited her on the south coast, where she lived with her daughter Dot, Dad's sister. These were mostly happy days spent with our cousins, who knew their uncle well. We tended to mix with extended family, as they knew of Dad's illness and gave Mum a bit of help. As kids, all through the 1960s and 70s, we cousins were like a swarm of bees travelling the neighbourhood, dropping in at houses to drink water from the hose or to pick whatever fruit hung over the fences. The only time we needed to be at home was before dinner or when the streetlights came on. Our cousins made an effort to laugh or snigger at Dad's silly antics when his mood was high.

On a couple of occasions, our father rang the ambulance in the early hours of the morning stating it was an emergency and relaying the need for them to go to Mum's mother's house – saying she had suffered a heart attack. Our maternal grandmother did in fact have a heart condition, which was probably worsened by Dad's practical jokes. Needless to say, the ambos were not impressed.

However, not long after his own mother's death, Dad once again slid into a major depression. He was back at home when the local police – who by now seemed like extended family – returned him to hospital. Dad's notes in regard to that admission say he was 'wandering aimlessly, appeared confused, chatting to himself and wanting to die'. From the medical records, Dad was also said to be 'garrulous, weepy, distressed… and he blames all his troubles on his wife'. After a few ECTs, his mood lifted, which was a signal for Dad to go AWOL once more.

Dad somehow hailed a taxi home, demanded the fare to pay the driver and announced to Mum he didn't need to go back. She notified the staff who, in turn, alerted the police to bring him back to the ward. Things were reaching an impasse at home for Mum, following Dad's bouts of agitation and delusional jealously leading to abusive and false accusations. This culminated in an intolerable state for Mum. She feared for her safety and finally moved to a rented flat.

Dad found this impossible to accept and went completely berserk. He was now on lithium carbonate to stabilise his moods. However, that combined with lots of alcohol, was mostly 'pissed out', as he'd say. He ranted, smashed things and attempted to find out where Mum was living. My siblings and I were accused of hiding her.

I was now living in a 1900s high-ceilinged house in Hunters Hill with a brick side access path leading to the entrance. It opened into a tiled foyer, which had five doors leading to bedrooms and the lounge area. It was around this time Dad arrived at my home in a drunken and frantic state. His grey eyes darkened to charcoal when he bashed the front door, believing I was Mum. I tried to tell him otherwise and explained Mum had left the family home for her safety. By this stage, Dad was enraged, pacing and banging doors in our foyer, looking into corners and pleading for Mum. When told to leave, Dad punched my husband into a wall so hard he broke his ribs, leaving him slumped and gasping.

Recollections of my childhood days, when I was powerless to demand the follow-up groups to leave our home, resurfaced. This time however, a primitive voice roared from deep within. I shrieked, 'Get out, get out…this is MY home.'

I'd had enough. Even my own home wasn't the sanctuary I'd imagined it would be. The police were called again. The scene unfolding around me was pitiful. Dad was hauled away muttering something about Mum, while my husband was bent over clutching his ribs, and I was bereft, sobbing.

My gratitude to the mental health services in those days was unwavering. Without Mum around to pick up the pieces, my brother and I (my sister was now interstate) relied heavily on the health services to look after our father. We visited frequently and helped him run his life by shopping, cleaning, washing and general chores. In due course, we had Dad's financial affairs put under the control of the Protective Office, as he was still suspicious toward Mum, and believed that because she was working full-time, he would have his pension revoked.

Our parents divorced some years later, yet in the end neither had any other partner in their lives. The years passed and Dad's illness became more chronic. He settled down on large doses of oral and long-acting intramuscular medication, along with community care. This kept him well enough to enable both parents to meet at various family gatherings – though to be on the safe side Mum never divulged her new address.

There were still some episodes, though, when Dad's normal mood fluctuated as he spiralled into a hypomanic state. This was the stage before he reached a full-blown manic episode, which required police to transport him to hospital. I usually visited, along with my brother, as we were next of kin, yet there were times when I felt overwhelmed.

At one stage when I was made aware by staff that Dad was still pacing and raving in the ward, I couldn't bring myself to drag my heavily pregnant body to the hospital. Much later, I read in Dad's file a note from late 1980: 'Daughter refuses to visit while her father in his current state…' I wasn't refusing outright, but at the time found I just couldn't keep up the visits. There was no mention that I was about to have my first baby in less than two weeks. After having worked as a health professional, I can now see the need to view these expectations within the broader context of relevant family issues.

Nonetheless, something shifted inside me. I wanted it all to end with Dad; it was too much to bear. I needed to disengage with him for my own sanity. Craving someone to share the burden of taking care of him, I absolutely appreciated the commitment and respite the health services gave Dad, and me.

15

The Ha Ha wall

Later in 1980, after my first baby was born, I visited my father, who was admitted into a locked ward at Gladesville Psychiatric Hospital. It wasn't the first time I had visited him. In fact, over the years, it was probably the thousandth time I had seen the inside of a psych ward. However, this was the first time I had taken a baby with me. Long gone were his days at private facilities, a therapeutic community ward and less secure open environments, which allowed day and weekend leave. This time, Dad was at the end of the road, the most secure ward for refractory and troublesome patients, many of whom had been long forgotten by family and friends.

His bipolar disorder and varying degrees of paranoia, along with addiction to alcohol and prescription drugs, all carried diagnostic labels. Over the years, it didn't really matter what the diagnosis was, as the torment, agitation, depression and mania all rolled into one as Dad's moods spiralled up and down. Eventually, he ended up locked away for periods of time, much to everyone's relief.

Before heading to the ward in the spring of 1980, I sat for a while at a nearby creek. A soft breeze caressed my face. Cradling my newborn, I fed her warm milk from my breast and watched her eyes glaze over with pleasure as her belly filled. After plucking a buttercup, I held the tiny flower under her chin, and watched her pale skin shine yellow. 'This means you will like butter one day,' I whispered as her eyes drooped shut. 'Time to go now, my little buttercup.'

I carried her up a hill towards the ward which, from the outside, seemed bordered by a one and a half metre sandstone wall. It can't be too bad in there, I thought, imagining the patients looking out through a tree-dappled view to Bedlam Bay. I rang the doorbell. Footsteps echoed as a nurse approached, keys jangling from a chain attached to her belt.

Passing through the double-keyed entrances and down the pastel-painted corridor leading into the ward, I was led to an open courtyard. It was spacious and dusty from pacing patients, leaving only a few grassy patches.

The nurse suggested the baby remain with the staff. I felt my grip tighten.

'Leave her with us for a bit. Things get a bit chaotic out there,' she warned.

'Dad would never harm her.' I hesitated at the thought of letting my baby go.

'Best to be on the safe-side – from the others in the ward.'

On hearing the screeching and scuffling in the background, I conceded perhaps she had a point. Reluctantly, I handed over my child.

In the distance, I saw my father striding the length of the courtyard whipping up dust in his wake while gazing beyond the sandstone wall to the bay, no doubt looking for an escape route. Momentarily the thought struck me: it was amazing he hadn't already jumped over such a low barrier to freedom. Over the years whenever he found himself captive, held against his will under the Mental Health Act, Dad babbled, 'Stone walls do not a prison make, nor iron bars a cage.'

Approaching, I forced a smile. 'Hi, Dad. Seems like you're planning to flee this place.'

'Have a look down there.' Dad pointed to the deep waterless moat on the inside of the sandstone wall.

Now I laughed in earnest. 'No wonder you didn't take a flying leap.'

'That's why they call it the Ha Ha wall, because every so often someone tries to escape and fails, then slides down into the moat.'

I later learnt quite a few of these Ha Ha walls still existed in old Victorian-era asylums in England and Australia.

'Come and sit down in the shade, Dad. It's too hot for pacing around.'

We found a couple of painted wooden-slat chairs under a willow tree near the high side of the moat.

Out of earshot of the staring patients, I questioned my father. 'Tell me what happened. How did the fire start?'

Dad's eyes flicked left and right as he scanned the area checking for hidden microphones, under the seat and near the tree. When satisfied it was safe to speak, he told his story. 'It was like this. I thought if I played the record over and over, your mother would come back. I turned it up loud, like I always do when I sing to her – to make sure she hears me wherever she is.'

Fed up, I sighed, hearing his singing along to loud music, as he used to when I lived in the family home.

My reverie was broken by Dad's nattering. 'Those bloody sticky-beak neighbours rang the coppers who came to the house and told me to turn it down. They warned me not to do it again or they'd lock me up.'

'You should know by now to keep out of their way.'

Unprompted, Dad burst into his favourite Ray Charles song: 'I can't stop loving you; I've made up my mind…'

'Stop, Dad! Listen to me. Exactly how did it happen?' I could see him winding up again, anxious to get an answer before he spun out of control.

'What? She bloody left. That's what happened.'

'No. The fire! How did it start?' With mounting irritation, I urged, 'We need to fill in the insurance papers so we can get the house fixed before you can live in it again.'

Unstoppable, Dad now had an audience from the other inmates. He stood tall as he sang and danced alone with his arms wrapped in the air as if he were holding his wife: 'Those happy hours that we once knew…'

The nurses entered the courtyard and tried to calm my father, who was now in full flight, ramping up his antics and encouraging the crowd to join in the singalong. Some mimicked his chorus. Another started to yell abuse at my father. Dad angrily pushed him away, and also shoved a dishevelled bloke who tried to steal his cigarette. While still singing, Dad grabbed a short lady with a basin haircut who was clothed in a drab floral dress. He proceeded to twirl her around and around until she shrieked to be released.

A hefty male nurse sauntered into the yard to break up the shenannigans. 'Settle down, mate. Come with me.'

'There's nothing wrong with me,' Dad said, pointing a finger at the female patient. 'I've already been attacked by that nymphomaniac woman eight times.' He started singing again.

'Dad, please stop singing,' I pleaded, eager to reach my baby girl, whom I heard crying from inside of the nurse's office. I was relieved she was away from the bedlam. 'I've got to go, the baby's upset.' Exasperated, I yelled, 'What really happened?'

'Maybe I emptied the ashtray in the kitchen bin, or left the radiator on and went to bed, that's all.' He laughed. 'The old buzzard next door smelled smoke and called the fire brigade.' As he was led by the elbow into a more isolated section of the ward, Dad added, 'He thought his place would burn down too.'

'Lucky he did make the call or you'd be dead by now. Most of the house is damaged.' Frazzled, I huffed toward the office.

'As if I wouldn't know how to put out a fire,' Dad muttered, before continuing relentlessly with his noisy chanting. 'I can't stop loving you…'

Shaking my head, I gave up and wandered back to the nurses office. What a crazy place this is, I thought. Greeted with a slip of a smile on my buttercup's face, I clutched her tight and escaped outside into a different world.

Years later when I subsequently visited the same old psychiatric hospital, I stopped at the sundial inside the Victoria Road gates. I read the inscription.

'Time wastes us, our body and our wits,
and we waste time so time and we are quits.'
(Anonymous, circa late 1800s)

When entering the grounds from a side-street gate, another sandstone building had at its front a tall clock tower, which chimed the daily routine for over a hundred years. I wrote this short piece.

Time keeping

Two timepieces stand across the bay
Both tell the time still to this day

The sundial squats on its grassy base
The clock tower stands to show its face

In daylight long shadows mark the time
The clock by night sounds its chime

As sunbeams wane below the land
Long arms of darkness seize time's hand

With crazy courage few dared escape
Past the sundial near the gate

Where etched upon its weathered stone
Are faded words from eras gone

16

Chimera

In the 1970s and 1980s, I was working in the mental health system after having previously completed a postgraduate psychiatric nursing course. Working in the environment felt very comfortable for me – probably because I'd spent so much of my life with craziness at home and visiting inpatient settings. The study and history of psychiatry over the ages, as well as multiple changes in the twentieth centur, fascinated me. I later went on to study sociology and anthropology and complete three university degrees, including my doctoral thesis as an ethnographic researcher on a deinstitutionalisation study.

When doing courses, the lectures which struck me most were those on anti-psychiatry. At the time, I read widely on the subject, as well as transactional analysis, gestalt and theories on double-bind communications, whereby conflicting messages are given in the same sentence, creating confusion and distress. The 1960s also saw the development of the anti-psychiatry movement in Britain, where relationships within the family, reflected in the wider society, were seen as a root cause of mental illness, whereby the 'sick' patient became a symptom of a 'sick society'. The first edition of the in-house newspaper from Fraser House also speaks to this point where at a family level,

> …it is shown that the patient is not the only one sick but is only the weakest link, and so is the first to break down. (Fraser House newspaper Vol. 1, No. 1, 1963)

As well, it was a time when families were mooted to have a causal role in the development of mental illness. For example, the term 'schizophrenogenic mother' was used, suggesting that schizophrenia was essentially attributable to parenting, more specifically the mother. Writers such as Laing, Cooper and Szasz had an impact on the UK psychiatric establishments, which filtered around the globe. This also included therapeutic communities where staff and residents worked alongside each other, sometimes with equal status on committees for decision-making in regard to day-to-day running of the ward, for example Kingsley Hall in London (R.D. Laing). This movement was reflective of an era where human rights were debated and injustices protested against. It was generally a more liberal time in society, which also coincided with the development of antipsychotic drugs, whereby some long-term institutionalised patients were able to move out for the first time in years.

The first therapeutic community of its kind in Australia, where Dad was a patient, encompassed a lot of what the movement was about in those days. However, in some instances, it developed further. Particular aspects included incorporating co-resident treatment for partners and families, an imbedded resident committee structure, where those involved helped govern the ward from a patient perspective, along with the setting and carrying out of rules for fellow inmates. The selection criteria for this ward was also experimental in the way it determined guidelines for a group of residents with opposite types of illness and behaviours, hoping the desirable aspects of some would influence other residents, to counteract negative behaviours. In theory, a lot of what was attempted was done with good intention; nonetheless, emotional damage to vulnerable people was also apparent.

Fraser House eventually closed as staff moved on and other practices developed. Some of the reasons it closed are related to criticism and political manoeuvring in regard to the director and practices. Other coinciding issues at the time, '…aimed at the relative devolution of Fraser House', were the development of an external therapeutic '[welfare] community' which took a lot of the developer/unit director's time, hence Fraser House planning and supervision of staff was delegated to the psychiatrist in charge. There was a 'temporary schism between both psychiatrist and developer (Unit Director of Fraser House) over the last couple of months' (February 1967).

There were also services developing at Gladesville Hospital, including a domiciliary nurse service and the setting up of the Tarban Project, later renamed the Tarban Clinic, and some staff movement between the two services.

The comment of the Director of State Psychiatric Services…on the development of Mental Health Centres over the next year or two provides a specific example of possible roles for the staff outside of the hospital.

Thus Fraser House, or at the State level, the growth of community psychiatry, appears to have passed through its first major change in its development, since the original concepts were begun at North Ryde. The Developer believes the events over the previous couple of months represent the transition from hospital therapeutic community to external welfare community, of which the Tarban project may well be the Australian prototype. (Yeomans, 1967: Confidential paper from State Library NSW)

Things were beginning to change in those days long before the Richmond Report (1983), Burdekin Report (1993) and subsequent reports, all of which impacted upon the development of mental health services and contributed to an ever-changing system.

It took some time for me to piece together what I had studied of this earlier phase in psychiatry when the therapeutic community operated. Fragments lost in my memory were reassembled or sometimes discarded. I recognised that what I had learnt was akin to my lived experience as a child with Dad and Mum in Fraser House.

Growing up, I was very connected to my family. As a child, you don't live in isolation, and consequently it defines you in many aspects. I tried to break the tether, yet it always pulled me back. Hanging over me was the constant comparison of our strange, often tormented family, with those families I thought were conventional. Perhaps my ideal of a normal family was nothing more than a chimera. I watched the *Brady Bunch* as a teenager and visited friends' homes where things seemed perfect. This left me exposed and vulnerable if ever I had to explain what went on in my home. I developed a way of avoiding questions and didn't say much, all the while shifting and adjusting my thoughts to neatly fit a response.

Later with my own kids, I set about creating a 'normal' family. Of course things are never really completely 'normal'. There are ups and downs, furies, sadness and sorrow, alongside extremes of happiness. I wondered and worried if I was able to achieve this given the turbulent years of my childhood. I was also watchful and alert to any idiosyncrasies in myself, and later my family, which might spark mental health problems. I know of no one else in our extended family who had any major mental illnesses. Nevertheless, I considered what, if any, characteristics of mental health issues had been inherited from Dad. Certainly there had been small bouts of treatable depression in some family members, though nothing major or debilitating. What I did inherit, along with my siblings, from Dad was a sense of humour, a tad of anarchy and a passion to support the underdog. My looks were more akin to my mother's side. In terms of other traits, I guess have always been determined, stoic and never give up. I pressed on and 'did my best', as Mum would say.

Not long after my first baby was born, we moved to Darwin for a couple of years. This was a huge break from visiting Dad, which was left primarily to my brother in those years, coupled with the constant care from health services. I was defining my own life at last.

Upon returning from the Northern Territory, I was pregnant with my second child – another little girl, born in 1983. We lived, worked, renovated and moved houses, before setting off with the girls to travel Europe in a VW Kombi van for five months. I wrote to Dad and called him occasionally, grateful my brother was around in Sydney.

Returning from overseas, I was pregnant again. My big baby boy was born in 1986. We settled down to family life and school for the kids. I visited Dad regularly at his home unit in Lane Cove, where I often needed to throw a tiny stone at his window to wake him or make him aware of my presence, as I didn't possess a key. He usually didn't hear the phone, as his radio or television was blaring as he sat in a vinyl chair next to the dining room table smoking and drinking – reminiscent of his days in our family home. The neighbours complained, of course, so I had to constantly remind him not to do it, or they would ring the police or the mental health community team.

When I dropped in, it was usually with one or two kids in tow. I didn't talk about my father's illness to them, as they were little and just saw him as a funny old man. They didn't find it anything out of the ordinary when I put the kettle on and simultaneously ran the kitchen sink full of sudsy water to wash the fat-splattered frypan and dishes, before heading to the bathroom to tackle the greyish grime. Dad's personal grooming was always pretty good, hair combed and clean-shaven, even though his musty clothes smelt of beer and cigarettes. After I sorted his place out, Dad gave the kids a vitamin C lolly from his jar on the kitchen windowsill. Off home we'd go until the next week, along with an overflowing basket of washing in my arms. I supposed one day when my children grew up, they would recognise the strangeness in their grandfather's behaviour and sayings. The time would come when I needed to explain Dad's history and illness.

I never did, though, because when my children were still quite young, aged nine, seven and four, my father died.

17

Dad's death

During the year before, leading up to Dad's death, some significant world events took place. One of the most unforgettable and disturbing incidents happened in 1989 on Dad's birthday, 4 June. The massacre at Tiananmen Square in Beijing of student protestors demonstrating the need for Chinese government democratic reform, freedom of the press and freedom of speech, was unjustifiable. These were notions which Dad believed belonged to everyone. As a great supporter of the underdog in some situations, he didn't hesitate yelling back at the television or radio. Dad always wanted to be free from whatever shackles bound him, both physically and within his own mind. Later in the same year, Dad witnessed another memorable event when the Berlin Wall fell in November, symbolising the end of the Cold War. Dad regularly watched the news, and seeing the stone, brick and concrete fall was dear to his own aspirations of escape. In 1990, less than a year later, my father died.

I'd helped Dad with weekly shopping and chores for the past decade while he lived alone, after Mum had moved away. In the end, though, it was Johnno who found him. He had a key to Dad's apartment and discovered him semi-conscious on the kitchen floor. Johnno called the ambulance, and Dad was rushed to hospital, a barely breathing mess.

This was not the first time Johnno had found our father in a precarious situation. There was the time with the hose attached to the car exhaust pipe stuffed into the vehicle's window. Johnno, aged twenty, was heading off for a university exam, when he realised he'd forgotten some important notes and came home just in time. It was a close call. There was another time when the family had arrived home to find Dad had been floating with bloodied wrists and dragged out of the Parramatta River, saved by the water police.

But this time it looked like it might be the final call. The usual domestic phone conversations followed as we rushed to see him before he gasped his last breath. Whatever the reason, each member of the family visited, probably just because it had gone on for so long we couldn't really believe it was the end of those tumultuous years. Dad would have found it heartening to know we were there as he neared the end of his life.

When I visited the emergency ward to take Dad some toiletries and the newly washed pyjamas I'd left near his front door – more about that later – he tried to speak. However, the words were distorted and slow in coming. I sat for a while thinking about…not much at all. The doctors and nurses did the talking, explaining that our father had suffered a massive stroke and, more than likely, might have another soon. Things looked grim.

I touched his hand and told Dad what time I'd be back the next day.

He managed to get a few words out. 'You're not leaving me here, are you?' he mumbled.

I left, not knowing then that they would be the last words he spoke to me, or anyone else for that matter. Strange how things go full circle, I thought. All his life, my father had favourite sayings and often repeated: 'Stone walls do not a prison make nor iron bars a cage.' Right until his last breath I knew Dad wanted to escape as he lay there yearning to be free, groaning at the impossibility of his situation. I can imagine him waiting for an opportunity, stifled by the watchful eyes of staff and his physical inability to do so.

The next day, as predicted, Dad experienced another massive stroke with a brain stem injury. This left him lingering in a coma for a day or so. With our Mum by his side, my brother and I, along with our spouses, ducked in and out until he passed away. Jane still lived interstate and didn't make it in time to see Dad, but arrived a couple of days later in readiness for the funeral.

The only person with Dad when he actually passed away was Mum. She had come to be with him when informed Dad's condition had deteriorated. Mum was there, as always, to relieve us so we could get back to our families for a while. She never left his side, which is how Dad would have wanted it to end. When our father's body was taken away, the staff handed Mum his wedding ring. He had never removed it in all those years.

It was a blessing when he died. I felt a weight lift from me. My whole life since early childhood had somehow been intertwined with and shaped by Dad's illness – his erratic mood swings, unpredictable rages, the shame of his everyday craziness.

When friends asked how my father died, I answered, 'A stroke.' It was a reprieve to say something ordinary, rather than from suicide, which I had feared many times in the past. I failed to add that his stroke was probably due to years of smoking, alcohol addiction and abuse of prescription drugs. This was my way of coping and skirting around difficult questions. It added to the many white lies I told friends throughout my life.

I hated and loved him at the same time. Even today I can't recall how much I cried when Dad died – maybe I didn't.

The funeral took place a week later, attended by a handful of friends and relatives plus Johnno, Jane and me, along with our spouses. Mum, who had loved him all her life, was there supporting all of us. She held an embedded sense of duty even though they had been separated for some years. I guess I never really recognised Mum's heartache and loss, because I was too intent on trying to lead my own life with three young kids who required my attention. It was reminiscent of times when, no matter what Mum had to cope with during the day – work, children, house and other chores – she would always take a couple of hours out to visit Dad in whatever hospital he was admitted into.

I listened to the hymn in the chapel, 'Amazing Grace'. It reminded me of Mum, and I recalled how she had driven at night through a raging storm, when the power had gone down and the roads were awash from blocked drains. At one point, her car, with dulled headlights, was almost swept from the bitumen. Nonetheless, her husband expected to see her, and she never let him down. I wished that our mother *had* let him down a bit more – we needed her too. Yet those words were never spoken.

At the wake, Johnno asked the loaded question. 'Liz, when did you leave the basket of washing near Dad's door?'

I paused before answering, imaging the layers of an artichoke being peeled back to get to the heart of the matter.

'It was Saturday evening, okay! I had to go out to dinner and we were running late, and you know he's going deaf.'

'Did you knock?'

'No, not then. It was the only time I didn't knock! I got sick of climbing through the bushes under his window.' I defended my actions, as I didn't have a door key. 'I always had to find a stone to throw to wake him up – his neighbours thought it was peculiar until I explained what I was doing.'

Other family members huddled closer and stared at me.

'I didn't expect him to die. I didn't kill him, for God's sake,' I stammered. 'I'm the one who got stuck doing everything for him. I've got three young kids of my own and this was my only night out in weeks. So, I made a mistake. I just couldn't bear the thought of going through all the commotion again and cleaning up his stinking kitchen and what about...'

'It's okay. Nothing would have saved him.' Mum put her arm around me.

'We know that, Mum,' Johnno barked. 'But on Monday afternoon when I called the ambos they said he'd been lying there for two days on the kitchen floor. He looked terrible when I found him. It's always me who finds him.'

'Poor Dad,' my younger sister Jane said.

'Maybe if they'd got to him sooner, he would have been okay.' Johnno said.

I remembered the game of 'Let's Kill Dad' and how I had won. With a twang of guilt, I uttered in despair, 'It's not my damned fault he's dead.'

The only keepsake I have of Dad, apart from photos, is a round antique lacquered box with a faded rose painted on top. He used to leave it on a table next to his bed and I now keep it in my office. It holds nothing of any monetary value, just odd bits of his memories – a fire brigade cloth shoulder patch from one of his jackets, a handful of tarnished brass buttons and studs with the NSW Fire Brigade emblem, a penny copper coin minted in 1928 (the year of his birth), a sixpenny Australian stamp with a sepia kookaburra picture, and a collection of keys, nails and tap washers.

18

Looking back

A spherical moon shone like a beacon through the window into my dark room. It was still high in the sky when I lifted the blind. I was glad there would be a couple more hours before I needed to get up. I tried to go back to sleep, yet a niggling feeling of wanting to know more kept me awake. I was going shopping with Mum in the morning and decided to ask her about those early days with Dad, things unspoken about for years. It was 2018.

Mum was ready and waiting, and now over ninety still stood relatively straight backed. Her eyes sparkled and I could see she'd been busy. Tapestry Christmas stockings, for the burgeoning number of great-grandchildren, were laid out on the bench. They required quite a lot of patience and keen eyesight, which she fortunately still has, and doesn't wear glasses.

On the way to the shopping centre, Mum looked straight ahead, reflexively ready to put her foot on the brake if I swerved too close or tailgated other cars. Old habits never die, I mused. Detouring past the hospital grounds where Fraser House used to be, I glimpsed her staring out the side window.

'Remember those days, Mum, when Dad was in there and they held those large group sessions?'

Provoked, Mum immediately voiced her opinion. 'I remember those Big Groups. I loathed them. Everyone was expected to talk.' She hesitated. 'One time, your father was asked to find something that annoyed him about his wife, me.'

Trying hard not to let my eyes drift from the road, I attempted to seem nonchalant. 'What did he say?'

'He couldn't think of anything,' Mum said, before adding, 'The group members thought he was protecting me, so they badgered him some more until he said, "Independent. She's too independent."'

Mum continued. 'I spoke up without being asked. I said, someone has to work and feed the family – so what's wrong with that!'

She then recollected how a nurse had interjected at the time, 'Rob sees it as a fault.'

Mum continued. 'Rob gave in and said, "It's not really a fault but that's all I can think to say. There's nothing wrong with her."'

I listened without speaking, whereupon my mother then explained how the group seamlessly latched onto something or someone else. This became a way to deflect the focus from one to another. Once they had found a fault, it had to be explored. Mum pointed out that she found this annoying and in some cases vindictive. At the time, she just wanted to get home to tackle the myriad of tasks required before she flopped into bed around midnight. She knew she would be up again at dawn to begin another day of children, breakfast chores, work, early dinner and visiting the hospital every evening at times when she was no longer a co-resident there with her husband.

'That sounds terrible, Mum.'

'Well, that's how it was,' Mum sighed. 'I felt embarrassed at how intrusive the groups were, picking each other's Achilles heels until they found something wrong. Silly things that would otherwise be forgiven or forgotten."

'What was the purpose? I asked.

'Maybe it was for the staff's entertainment,' my mother grinned.

The group scenarios which I'd heard from my mother's perspective shed light on how harrowing it must have been for such a private person like her to be exposed in those situations, and still so clearly recollect them at her age. Mum wasn't bitter, though she was still a bit perplexed as to why the groups operated in that way.

The question, which hung over Mum and the rest of the family for years, was never really answered. However, Mum, now aged ninety-one, did try and understand it and penned a few thoughts, which are copied below.

> What went wrong – what caused the problem! Rob dislocated his shoulder coaching kids in soccer and at the time the stress of not working, mortgage, wife, three kids all caused his nerves to crack up, and from then on it was a constant battle of nerves and hospitalisations. Finally the kids all married and went their own ways. After a lot of quarrelling and abuse I left, we divorced and both lived alone, Rob until his death in 1990, and I am still on my own. Neither of us ever wanted another partner but life together was unbearable.
>
> I don't think it necessary to go into the details of the years of misery, drinking, upset childhoods of our children, just say nature is kind and one remembers the good times best. I can certainly say I had the worst and best of it in one marriage. I think I should add here that my children were always supportive of both of us after our divorce and have grown up, after their own 'wild times' to be sensible, responsible and caring parents and citizens.

A constellation of emotions overwhelmed me. I was left feeling somewhat bereft. Nonetheless, I was also prompted by thoughts of going back there sometime soon to try and sort out what it all meant. It was at that point that I decided to access old medical records from Dad's admissions. Ploughing through over twenty years' worth of notes, episodic memories from highly charged emotional events came to the fore. I was surprised how accurately my early childhood reminiscences were clarified in the pages of medical notes.

19

Bittersweet

Swatting a mozzie, I muttered to myself. 'Take that!' Roaming at dusk, I marvelled how the twilight closed the day, when the pink glow of sunset diminished and what photographers call 'the blue hour' lifted in the eastern sky. Soon it would be dark.

I recalled a quote from my great-grandmother. 'What is this world so full of care if we have no time to stand and stare?' (William Henry Davies, 1871–1940)

Instead of rushing home, after going through more of Dad's files in the medical records department of the hospital, I sat.

I gazed up the hill towards the vacant ward, which was once Fraser House. I pictured my birthday cake in 1966 in the grounds of the psychiatric hospital, which brought back feelings of a distant past. It was now over five decades since my lifetime wish was initially made when I blew out those candles. Scents of spring freesias wafted from the banks of the creek bed near some of the remaining willow trees. Recollections of those days were triggered like a flash bulb, illuminating situations not thought about for a long while.

Throughout life, I had 'thanked my lucky stars', as Nan would say. However, just to be on the safe side, I still made the same wish whenever blowing out candles – this year quite a few. Over time, I'd never exposed my wish to anyone – even though it was pretty standard one – in case it didn't come true. A silly superstition to live your life by, I thought. Nevertheless, I kept it hidden. It took a lot to uphold my secret, especially every year when I was asked; 'What did you wish for?'

People had commented in my adult years on what a lucky person I was; some even envied my somewhat charmed life. Only I knew what lay beneath my days full of love and laughter. Others didn't notice that my elation was tainted with a despondency which seeped into every crevice of my happiness. The expected spontaneity of delight in everyday occurrences was clouded by an inflated sense of foreboding. This acted as a constant unsettling reminder for me of how things might go belly-up in an instant. My anticipation, so clearly distinct, was often distorted by flatness and apprehension as I foresaw an ominous aftermath. So, when the boundaries of joy became blurred, in my mind I'd instantaneously rework the scene to construct a strategy for whichever scenario might eventuate, ready to handle any disappointment. Notwithstanding this, I relished the heightened anticipation before events, which for me was like biting into the sweet tangy taste of a passionfruit straight from the vine.

One such time as a child was before a family holiday at Kosciusko National Park to see the snow for the first time. The expectation of the trip was exhilarating. I chose my clothes, along with wool for the beanie Mum would knit each of us, while we read picture books about snowy places. When the family finally set off on the journey and were two-thirds of the way there, our father called an abrupt halt to the trip upon reaching Canberra. 'Too bloody cold, we're going home.' And that was that.

Another attempt at a family excursion, mentioned previously, was a day at the beach. Excited, packed and ready to go, we children grabbed our cossies and sand buckets while waiting for Dad to arrive home. The outing was soon called off after Dad ran over and killed our neighbour's dog. One more instance when we cringed and retreated indoors to watch the television. We had never owned a dog, but hearing the soft purr from our cat Whisky as I stroked his silky black and white fur left me wondering how sad the kids across the road were feeling without Banger.

What occurred some months later was unexpected. Dad arrived

home with a very large brown dog – I think he won it in a bet at the pub. My siblings and I were ecstatic as we played ball with him in the backyard, before he went to sleep on the veranda. Thrilled when school ended the next day, I skipped all the way to our front gate, eager to see our new dog – which had remained nameless at this point. Entering through our front door, things were unusually quiet and still – no barking or jumping. Dread lurched in my stomach. We soon heard the news. Dad had accidently let him out and, while off the lead, the bounding half-grown hound bolted to the busy road at the top of our street. Our dog was killed instantly in the traffic. We'd had him barely twenty-four hours, yet I still wanted to hear his bark, touch his wet nose and watch his canine twists as he chased Whisky, getting a scratch on the nose for his effort – I longed to lose myself in our dog's amber eyes.

A culmination of childhood commotion, usually coupled with wrath, influenced my feelings of tension as an adult whenever faced with joyful situations.

Reflecting upon more events of those chaotic years in the family home, such as fires, violence, suicide attempts and general upheaval, I can now understand why I periodically wanted to run away. Maybe it was just my version of 'the Great Escape', as our father called it. Sometimes the need to runaway was compelling – but where to and what from?

I chuckled remembering the very first time I ran away from home in 1959 – before the two teenage instances. I was nearly five years old and stamped my feet at some or other perceived injustice coming my way. I couldn't quite recall what it was, though knew it must have been pretty big to make me grab my teddy and stuff it in my tiny blue cardboard case with the metal buckle.

I stormed to Mum. 'I'm running away and you can't stop me. I'm not living here any more.'

Johnno and Jane hung in the background, enthralled by my antics as they watched the scene play out from the front porch.

Mum had learnt to be cool under pressure. Without saying anything, she followed my small steps up the driveway to the street. Mum planted a farewell kiss on my forehead, and then placed a banana in my bag along with a shilling coin in my pudgy hand before she spoke. 'That should do you for a while until you get a job.'

Accepting the offering, I ventured outside the gate – alone –for the first time in my life. About a hundred metres down the footpath – making sure I didn't step on the cracks – I stopped. Looking back to my house, I could see no one. I was frightened and thinking of monsters and scary things. I ran back as fast as I could, through the gate and into my mother's waiting arms. Bliss. Of course, she'd been surreptitiously watching all along.

My memories – or the impact of those memories, even though perhaps a tad foggy – were shaped by reactions to events, and consequently became a source of survival. Memory, often slippery, would pull its head back into a rock cave like an eel, and at other times slither through the maze of undertows as it shifted and twisted where time became distorted. Minutes seemed like days.

I drew strength from my memories to even out life's craggy contours. The ride was never smooth. Often, all I hoped for was nothing but a plan to get through each day until night-time, when I could close my eyes and dream of the faraway islands where the flightless cormorant has adapted to its environment, a place where its wings are no longer used for flying. Instead, the cormorant uses its wings to buffer wind currents and provide balance for landing from one rock to another.

In harnessing personal familiarity of dire situations, my rutted edges of happy experiences became clear. I always tried to dive through the waves of gloom before they washed over. Refusing to allow life to be defined by childhood years of chaos and trauma, I mobilised the feistiness I'd had as a young girl. This, I might add, was not so defined by my parents and others, who, more often than not, described me as insolent or wilful. Nevertheless, I clutched at an innate enthusiasm, which led to action, rather than hopelessness, which so easily could have stifled my life plan.

In the end, my dream had come true. Determined, I made sure it did. However, there was always something missing – this was evident each time my heart splintered, when I felt robbed of the full essence of joy.

> Stone walls do not a prison make
> Nor iron bars a cage:
> Minds innocent and quiet take
> That for an hermitage.
> If I have freedom in my love,
> And in my soul am free,
> Angels alone, that soar above,
> Enjoy such liberty.

(Richard Lovelace, 1642 – last stanza of poem 'To Althea, from Prison')

References and Notes

Chapter 1. A strange place
Clark, A.W. and N. Yeomans (1965). *Observations From an Australia Therapeutic Community.* Neville T. Yeomans, Collected Papers, 1965, Vol. 12, Sydney

The Sun newspaper, 1965, from State library NSW

Woman's Day, 1965, from State library NSW

Macquarie Hospital *Medical Records Department.* (These are my father's records, which are referred to in most chapters. There are about 25 years' worth from North Ryde Psychiatric Centre/Fraser House now renamed Macquarie Hospital and Gladesville Hospital.)

Macquarie Hospital Library

Chapter 7. In the firing line
DSM 5: American Psychiatric Association. (2013). *Diagnostic and statistical manual of mental disorders* (5th ed.).

Chapter 8. My birthday wish
Clark, A.W. and N. Yeomans (1965). *Observations From an Australia Therapeutic Community.* Neville T. Yeomans, Collected Papers, 1965, Vol. 12, Sydney.

Chapter 16. Chimera
Fraser House newspaper, Vol. 1, No. 1, 1963, from State library NSW

State Library NSW, Confidential paper of N. Yeomans. 24 February 1967: *A Community developer's thoughts on the Fraser House Crisis*

Cooper, D. *Anti-Psychiatry*, Penguin, Harmondsworth. UK. 1967

Laing, R.D. *The Divided Self.* Tavistock, London, 1960

Laing, R.D. *The Politics of Experience and the Bird of Paradise*, Penguin Books, Harmondsworth, UK 1975

Szasz, T. *The Myth of Mental Illness*, Paladin, Frogmore, St Albans, Granada. 1972

Szasz, T. *The Manufacture of Madness: A Comparative Study of the Inquisition and the Mental Health Movement*, Frogmore, St Albans, Granada. 1973

Richmond Report: chaired by David Richmond. *Inquiry into Health Services for the Psychiatrically ill and Developmentally Disabled* 1983 NSW

Burdekin Report: chaired by Brian Burdekin, *Human Rights and Mental Illness,* Volumes 1 & 2. AGPS, Canberra, 1993

Acknowledgements

I wish to thank those who helped me finish this memoir, including friends and family who have reviewed it and offered slight changes along the way.

The Common Thread writing group have always provided support, critical appraisal and encouragement.

I also acknowledge Patti Miller and her wonderful memoir-writing course along with her book *Writing True Stories*, which gave me the tools to carry on and structure the memoir.

Many thanks to Caroline Baum for reviewing and shaping the timeline, her kind words to keep me going, and suggestions for the final title.

Thank you to the staff at the Macquarie Hospital Medical Records Department and Library, who have been invaluable in locating my father's records covering many years and admissions.

I also acknowledge the staff of the State Library NSW for their expertise and thoroughness in locating old papers and articles.

Finally, as this memoir is the story of my childhood life, which shaped to a large extent the adult I would become, I thank my family. I am indebted to my mother, who shared her love and memories of good and bad times, our father who cherished us and, even though his illness was ever present, provided us with valuable life lessons and phrases which set the groundwork for a lasting resilience. My brother and sister of course were always there and still are, as we share our lives with children and grandchildren.

My dream of course would never have come true without my own children and husband.

www.ingramcontent.com/pod-product-compliance
Lightning Source LLC
Chambersburg PA
CBHW070918080526
44589CB00013B/1352